GROSSOLOGY and YOU

by Sylvia Branzei

illustrated by Jack Keely

PSS!
PRICE STERN SLOAN

Acknowledgments

*This book is dedicated to Byron and to George,
our biggest fans and our most honest critics.
—S.B. and J.K.*

Library of Congress Cataloging-in-Publication Data
Branzei, Sylvia.
    Grossology and you / by Sylvia Branzei ; illustrated by Jack Keely.
       p. cm.
    Summary: Provides information in a not-so-serious manner about such topics as blood, eyeballs, brains, bruises, constipation, warts, rashes, and more.
       1. Human physiology—Juvenile literature. 2. Body, Human—Juvenile literature. 3. Body fluids—Juvenile literature. [1. Human physiology. 2. Body, Human.] I. Kelly, Jack, ill. II. Title.
    QP37.K295   2002
                                                                                                        2002003636

ISBN 0-8431-7736-5   2010 Printing

PSS!® and Grossology® are registered trademarks of Penguin Putnam Inc.

And Now a Message from Our Corporate Lawyer:

Neither the publisher nor the author shall be liable for any damage that may be caused or sustained as a result of conducting any of the activities in this book without specifically following the instructions, conducting the activities without proper supervision, or ignoring the cautions contained in the book.

GROSSTENTS

A GROSS INTRODUCTION

Gross is in the eye
of the beholder.

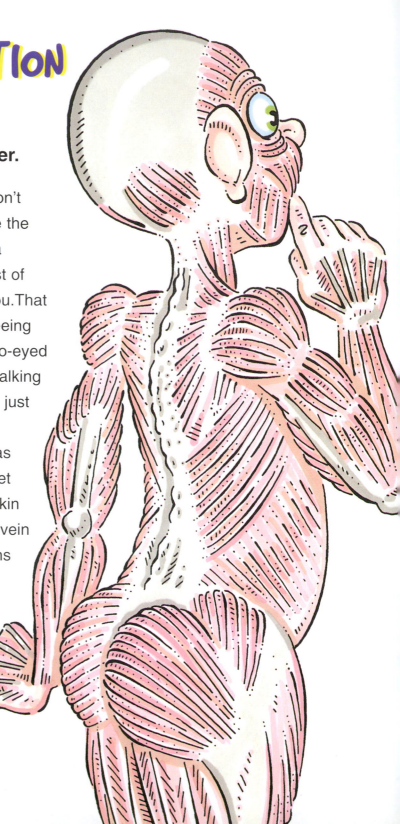

When you see people, they don't disgust you. Except for maybe the bratty kid next door who has a constant snotty nose. So, most of the time people don't revolt you. That is because you are used to seeing skin covered, lightly furred, two-eyed beings. If you saw a person walking down the street with no skin, just a bunch of blood covered muscles, you would think it was yucky. However, if everyone walked down the street as a bag of muscles, you would probably think a skin person was really icky. The same thing goes for a vein woman or a skeleton kid or an entrail man. Humans are accustomed to looking at the outside of our bodies. When you get to the insides, it gets oozy, goopy, sticky, and stinky.

It is not pleasant.

That's gross. No, this is gross. What's gross? One person's grossness can be another person's dinner. Fried grasshoppers are a delicious treat eaten in Australia, Africa, Japan, and other parts of Asia. They are popped and crunched much like North Americans eat peanuts. So, if you lived in fried grasshopper eating areas, it wouldn't be weird. And fried grasshopper eaters might think that a tube stuffed with pig lips and snouts (otherwise known as a hot dog), is a revolting meal. Like fashion, what's gross changes with the times. In the Middle Ages, people thought that taking a bath was bad for you. It was not in fashion. Not needing to bathe was considered a sign of wealth and leisure. Some rich people bragged about never having taken a bath. **Smelly!** Now it is quite the opposite. Nowadays people not only bathe, they deodorize, and perfume themselves. Being stinky is not in fashion.

So, you may read some things in this book and find them completely repulsive. But when you tell your cousin about it, he or she may say, "What's so gross about that?" Then again, some things you don't find so bad, your cousin won't even be able to look at on the page. That is the joy of **Grossology**. Everyone has a personal gross button and you never know whose you will hit.

BLOOD

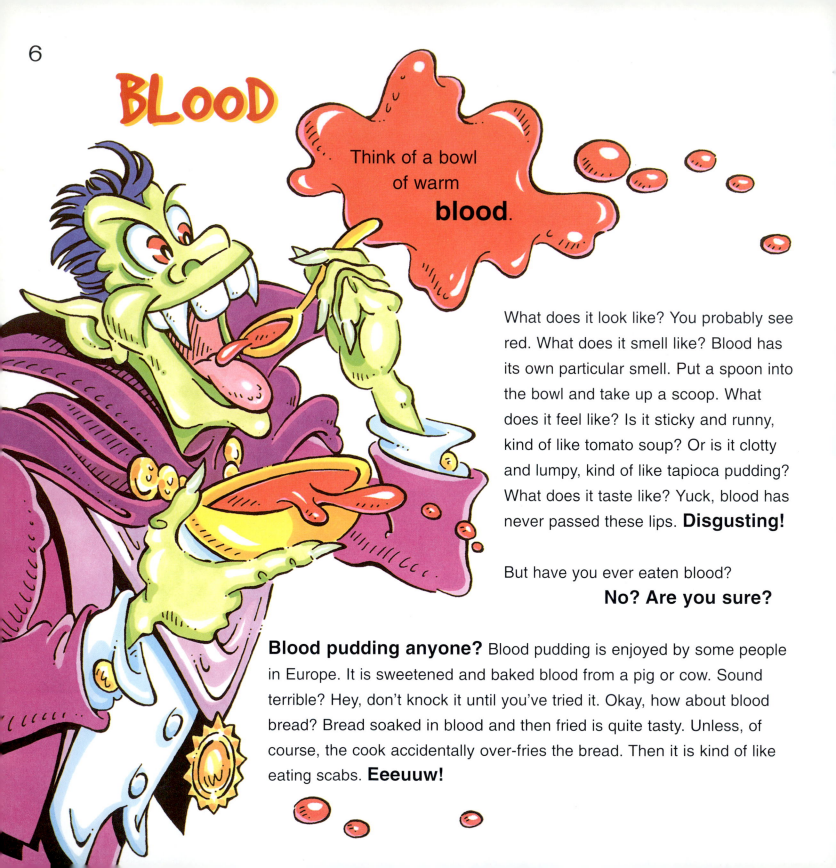

Think of a bowl of warm **blood**.

What does it look like? You probably see red. What does it smell like? Blood has its own particular smell. Put a spoon into the bowl and take up a scoop. What does it feel like? Is it sticky and runny, kind of like tomato soup? Or is it clotty and lumpy, kind of like tapioca pudding? What does it taste like? Yuck, blood has never passed these lips. **Disgusting!**

But have you ever eaten blood?
No? Are you sure?

Blood pudding anyone? Blood pudding is enjoyed by some people in Europe. It is sweetened and baked blood from a pig or cow. Sound terrible? Hey, don't knock it until you've tried it. Okay, how about blood bread? Bread soaked in blood and then fried is quite tasty. Unless, of course, the cook accidentally over-fries the bread. Then it is kind of like eating scabs. **Eeeuuw!**

How about mashed potatoes with gravy? **Yummm.** If you have eaten mashed potatoes and gravy, you have tasted blood. No, not the potatoes, the gravy. A recipe for gravy will say, "take the meat juice, add flour, heat and stir until thick." Well, "meat juice" is actually animal blood and melted fat. So, gravy is cooked blood. If you order steaks rare, you have also tasted blood.

If you weigh 100 pounds, you are carrying around eight pounds of blood.

YUMMY.

When you thought of a bowl of blood, you probably pictured a red liquid. Less than half of your blood is actually made of red blood cells, or erythrocytes (eee-RITH-row-sites).

The rest is white blood cells, platelets, and plasma—the liquid that blood cells float around in. Erythrocytes are so tiny that 7,000 of them could fit on the edge of a penny. One teaspoon of blood has 25 billion red blood cells. That's more red blood cells than there are people living on the planet. In your whole body, you have thirteen soda cans of blood! That's more red blood cells than all the people who have ever lived on this planet.

Blood is thicker than water. Blood is also heavier than water.

The red in red blood cells is from a pigment called **hemoglobin**. *Hemo* comes from the Greek word for "blood." The hemoglobin pigment has iron molecules. The same iron metal used to make cannon balls and frying pans. There's only a teeny tiny amount of iron in blood, though, so that you don't become weighted down from carrying it. When iron meets **oxygen**, a **gas**, it makes **red rust**. The same is true for blood. It is the oxygen combining with the iron in blood that makes it red. The hemoglobin cruises around your body and exchanges much needed oxygen for useless **carbon dioxide**. Talk about a recycling system!

After the red blood cells make their oxygen delivery, they change color and become more purple. The blood in your veins looks blue or purple because they carry **erythrocytes** without oxygen—rust-free blood.

After about 100,000 trips around your body, red blood cells get old. Red blood cells only live for about two months because they get bumped and bruised while traveling through the blood vessels. So, the blood cell retires. Then your body gets rid of it or uses it to make new red blood cells. Since **erythrocytes** are so important, new ones are constantly made. Many bones inside your body contain blood factories, like the bones of your arms, legs, ribs, hips, and back. The blood factories never stop. **An adult body makes about two million new red blood cells every second!** And you thought bones just held your muscles.

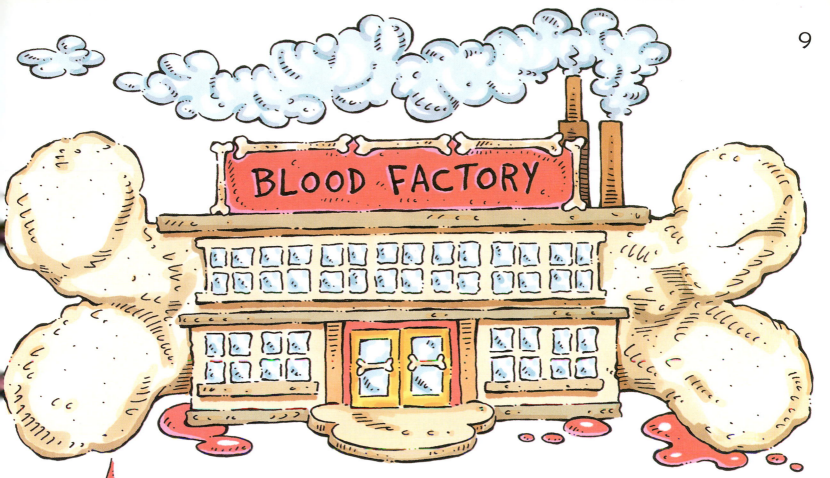

Quick! What color are white blood cells?

Duh, white? Exactly. If red blood cells are the delivery and recycling system of the body, the white blood cells or **leukocytes (LOU-koh-sites)** are the soldiers. Your body has a built-in military, and it's a good thing because your body is always under attack. **Bacteria, mold, viruses, pollutants, dirt, and splinters are just some of the enemies the white blood cells destroy.** Since not all attacks are the same, not all leukocytes are the same either. One type of white blood cells are called **Feeding Cells. Feeding cells do exactly that, they eat the invaders.** They are like mobile blobs squeezing through the walls of the blood vessels and attacking. Feeding cells can only eat so much before they become poisoned and they die. Basically, they eat themselves to death.

People used to think that bad blood was the cause of most diseases. The cure was to cut the patient and drain out the bad blood.

Macrophages (MAC-row-fages) are large, compared to the feeding cells, and have giant appetites. Macrophages eat the slain piles of bacteria, dead feeding cells, and debris in the body's battle-field. The body militia also has another line of defense. These fighters are like the special forces. They search and destroy. They are called **killer cells**. On top of all this is an intelligence unit that remembers every attack and makes special proteins to fight the enemy. That is why you don't get the mumps or chicken pox twice. Every time you get the flu, it is a new virus. If you get exposed to an old flu, the intelligence unit will wipe it out before you get sick.

When you get a small cut or wound your body looks out for you. It will take about four to eight minutes for your body to halt the bleeding. Then a dried-blood cover will form over the cut. **This job falls to the fix-it crew or platelets that barricade the ouchy area.** Platelets flow along with the blood, but in the face of danger they change. They become sticky and clump together forming a plug that stops blood from leaking. Ever touch a cut after a few minutes? The blood becomes jellylike, thick, and goopy. **The gooey blood is a clot**. The clot puts out threads that criss-cross to form a net. When the surface of the clot dries, it forms a scab.

In England, the word "bloody" is considered a bad word.

Fake Blood

What you need:
Cornstarch, red food coloring,
powdered cocoa, corn syrup
(used for cooking, not for pancakes),
water, a bowl, a spoon, and a measuring cup.

What you do:
Place ¼ cup of syrup and 2 teaspoonfuls of water
into the bowl. Stir well.

Add 4 drops of red food coloring. Stir.
Add 2 teaspoonfuls of cornstarch and ½ spoonful of powdered cocoa to the mixture.

Stir very, very, very well.

Put on clothes that you don't care about at all. (The blood will stain your clothing.)

Drip the blood from the side of your mouth. Or better yet, put some in your mouth.
(It is not harmful, but it doesn't taste too great either.)

Go find an unsuspecting person (like your little brother or sister), and say,
"I vant to suck your blood."

Blood cells float around in a river of **plasma (PLAZ-ma)**. This yellow liquid is mostly water, but it also contains fats, sugars, salts, gases, albumin (which is found in egg whites), and urea which also makes up pee. So, in one teaspoon of blood there are 25 billion red blood cells, 35 million white blood cells, and a billion platelets. All of this floats in the plasma soup.

PUS

The scientific word for pus is **pus**.

There is just no other word for it. Pus is foul. Pus is stinky. Pus is putrid. Pus is infection. Pus is pus. Saying the word pus sounds like you have a mouthful of it. How yummy.

Pus, pus, pus and blood. Pus and blood go together. Without blood there would be no pus. If you read the section on blood, you know how important blood is. You can't do without blood. **Pus just comes along as a side effect when bacteria invade.** The bacteria are in search of a nice, warm place to live and multiply. Your body is a perfect place to raise the family. Food is easy. The weather is perfect. The only problem is that the body doesn't like bacteria taking up residence, so it sends in the troops, or white blood cells.

Certain white blood cells, called phagocytes (FA-goh-sites) just love the taste of bacteria, dirt, and dead liquified body tissue.

"Phag" actually means to engulf, and that is just what these cells do.

They eat and eat and eat. And then they die.

More phagocytes arrive and they feast on bacteria, dirt, tissue, and their dead friends. The dead stuff builds up to make yellowish, greenish, whitish pus. All of the teeny tiny dead stuff also makes pus stink.

Eventually white blood cells win the battle, the body cleans up the pus, and everything is back to normal once again. Hooray! But occasionally, the body may need some assistance to win. Antibiotics kill off bacteria to help infections heal more quickly.

Just a little bit of pus isn't so bad. A small amount of pus in an area is called a **pustule** (how cute). Sometimes zits will get infected. The whitehead of the pimple turns a bit yellow.

Yup, zit material mixed with bacteria equals pus—or to be more accurate, a pustule.

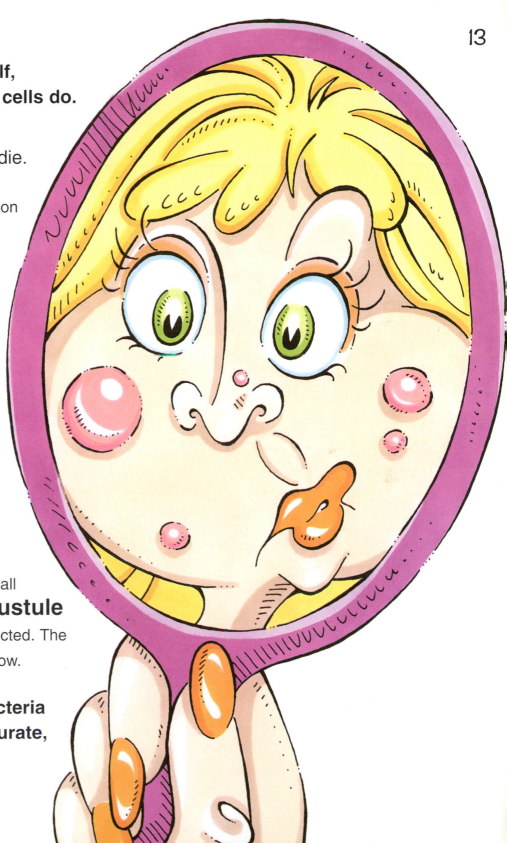

Abscess. **Another lovely word.**

Abscess sounds like it should go along with pus and it does.

A whole collection of pus in an area is an abscess. **Basically, it is a pool of pus.**

Sometimes the pus from an abscess works its way to the surface of the skin. Sometimes it dumps into other parts of the body. Pus pools can show up almost anywhere. You can get an abscess in your ear, on your butt, in your brain, or on your bowel. But it occurs most often in the root of a tooth. An abscessed tooth may have to be removed, or for just as much fun, the tooth's nerves pulled out. Dentists call this a root canal. Mention the words root canal around adults and you will notice shivers and frowns. A root canal is *not* fun, but then having a pus-filled pocket is no fun either.

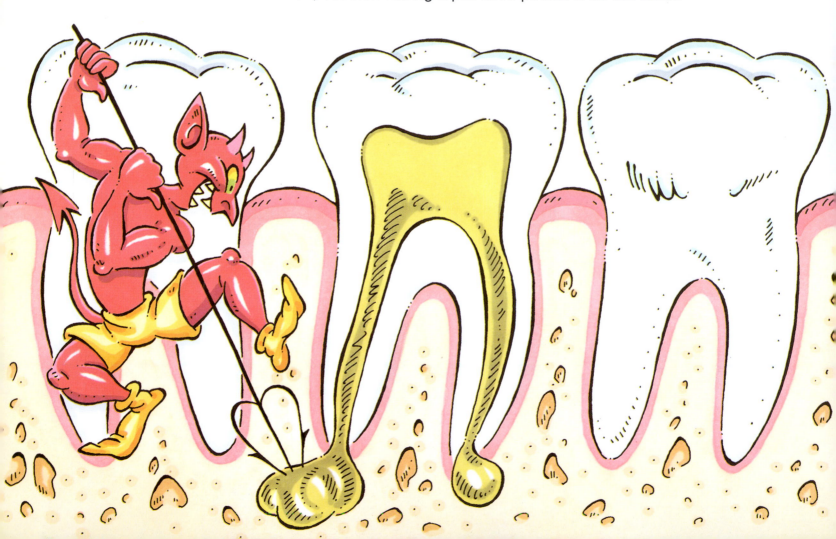

Maggots love rotting meat. Before there were antibiotics, maggots were sometimes used to clean up pus-filled wounds. Munch, munch. All clean!

For more pus-filled excitement, there are boils. Boils are pus-filled bubbles that form when a bunch of pus gets trapped under the skin. Maybe it got the name boil because it looks like a bubble. But don't burst your bubble, or rather boil. The living bacteria inside the boil can spread the infection to other people, or even into your bloodstream. Sometimes boils will burst all on their own, and that is good. The yucky pus that comes out should be cleaned up. If the boil just gets big and red and hot, it is time to see a doctor. The doctor gets to have the fun job of lancing the boil or busting the pus-filled bubble and draining the pus out of it.

SNEEZE

ACHOO!

"God bless you."

Back in the Middle Ages, people thought that when you sneezed, your soul came flying out and wandered for a bit. If the devil was in the area, your soul could be snatched. However, if someone said, "God bless you," your soul would safely return to your body.

This superstition may sound fantastic but what really happens when you sneeze is almost as scary. **A sneeze projects millions of tiny snot droplets, from the mouth and the nose, at speeds greater than a racing horse.** The snot drops float through the air, land on everything, and are inhaled by anyone nearby. This really isn't so bad since snot is mostly water, salt, and protein. Okay, a snot shower is not a very pleasant experience. **But it is worse if the sneezer has a cold or the flu.**

A sick sneezer coats you with nose **mucus** and **viruses** that can make you sick. Actually, doctors think that people probably get colds more from their own hands than from breathing the sneeze air. The sneeze gooby lands on your hands, then you stick a piece of gum into your mouth. It's the sneezy, germy gum that makes you sick.

The great snot rocket is actually due to teeny tiny little hairs called cilia (SILLY-a). The hairs act like a mucus escalator that moves dirty snot to the back of your throat. There are more cilia in one inch of your sinus than people at a World Series game. Cilia are very sensitive. If they get disturbed, they alert the nerves and the nerves alert the sneeze center in the brain. The brain tells you to stop breathing normally, to suck in air, to close off your mouth with the tongue, to blast air and snot through the nose, and to quickly relax the tongue so the nose spew is followed by a mouth snot shower. The force of the air blasts out whatever was bugging the cilia.

Super Sneeze Superstitions

One sneeze, make a wish.

Two sneezes, you will be kissed.

Three sneezes, you will be disappointed.

Four sneezes, expect a letter.

Five sneezes, you will get something new.

Six sneezes, you will take a trip.

Sneeze before breakfast, you will receive company before bedtime.

Sneeze three times before breakfast, bad luck.

You cannot keep your eyes open when you sneeze.

Anything that aggravates the nose can cause sneezing, such as pepper, dust, pollen, cold drafts, pet dander, smoke, and light. Light? Yup, about two percent of people have sneezing fits when they see bright light. In some people sneezing fits can be triggered by eyebrow plucking, hair combing, and even eating too much.

"That was a great meal . . . *Achoo!*"

Some people say that you can stop a sneeze. No, do not hold your nose shut. That's bad, very bad. Instead, use a finger to press hard on the midline between your upper lip and your nose.

Sternutation (stir-new-TAY-shun) is a very fancy word for a sneeze or the act of sneezing. A sternutator is not a sneezer but something that causes sternutation.

Although many sneezes don't carry germs, covering your mouth is still a kind thing to do when you sneeze. If you have a cold you might consider the safety sneeze, which is sneezing into your arm at your elbow rather than into your hands. That way you don't spread the infected snot by shaking hands with your principal, although giving Grandma a big hug after a safety sneeze is not a good idea. Or better yet, carry a tissue!

Snot for Sneeze

What you need:

⅛ cup of Borax laundry booster (no other detergent will do), ½ liter of warm tap water, a small container of Elmer's glue (no other kind will do), water, green food coloring, a clean, empty 1 liter soda bottle, a cup, and a spoon.

What you do:

Prepare the Borax solution. Place ⅛ **cup of the Borax laundry booster** into a ½ **liter of warm water**. Shake until most of the Borax dissolves. (Not all of it will dissolve.) Let the solution cool.

Pour ½ **cup of the Elmer's glue** into a bowl.

Add ½ **cup of water**. Stir.

Add **2 drops of the green food coloring**. Stir well.

Measure **8 spoonfuls of the Borax solution**.

Stir until the mixture looks clumpy. You can add another spoonful of the Borax solution if the snot is too runny.

Remove your snot.

Fake a sneeze, ACHOO!

Then show your friend how much snot came out of your nose.

ATHLETE'S FOOT

Is the skin between your toes red, flaky, and itchy?

You might have athlete's foot.

Does the skin crack open, crumble, and weep disgusting liquid? You might have athlete's foot. Do you have little blisters on the soles and sides of your feet? You might have athlete's foot. Is the top layer of skin white and soggy? You might have athlete's foot. Are your feet smelling especially foul? You might have athlete's foot.

And what you might have? Ringworm of the foot, A.K.A. athlete's foot, or as a doctor might say, tinea pedis.
Ringworm of the foot is not a worm at all. It is a type of fungus that likes to invade the upper layer of skin. Sometimes this fungus causes circular patches or crusty white lines on the skin.

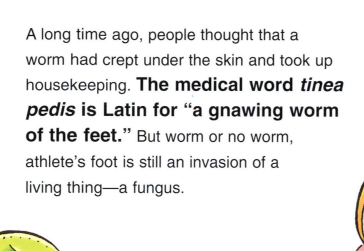

A long time ago, people thought that a worm had crept under the skin and took up housekeeping. **The medical word *tinea pedis* is Latin for "a gnawing worm of the feet."** But worm or no worm, athlete's foot is still an invasion of a living thing—a fungus.

I'll never go bowling again! Not to worry, bowling shoes are sprayed with a fungus killer.

The fungus prefers to take residence between your fourth and fifth toes. It puts down its roots into the outer layers of skin. The roots branch out as the creeping mold feeds on the protein, called **keratin (CARE-a-tin)** that makes up part of your skin. Warmth and moisture keep the fungus really happy. So, keep on running in those tennis shoes with no socks or with synthetic socks. Oh yeah, and don't wash your feet. Foot-rot heaven.

Hey, if you are really lucky and you are a boy, you might even get the athlete's foot fungus to spread to the area where your private parts are. This is called jock itch. Often athlete's foot and jock itch go hand and hand. This could be due to spreading the fungus as you dry with a towel. And the groin is paradise for the fungus—hot and moist.

Wait! Jock itch and athlete's foot? Does this fungus only attack people who like to play sports? Yes and no. Every seven out of ten people will get athlete's foot in their lifetime. However, it is more common in teenagers and adult males. When people play sports they sweat, they wear unventilated shoes, they walk barefoot in communal showers, and they get athlete's foot. **So, yes, the fungus shows up more often in athletic people.**

No one knows why, but fungus just like some people more than others. Researchers have tried to spread athlete's foot to volunteers by using the fungus, but they didn't have much luck. (Join the fight against athlete's foot. Volunteer today). So, while your friend may be able to wander at the public pool and stay fungus free, you could go shoeless and infected skin flakes or fungal babies, called spores, grab hold of your feet and take over.

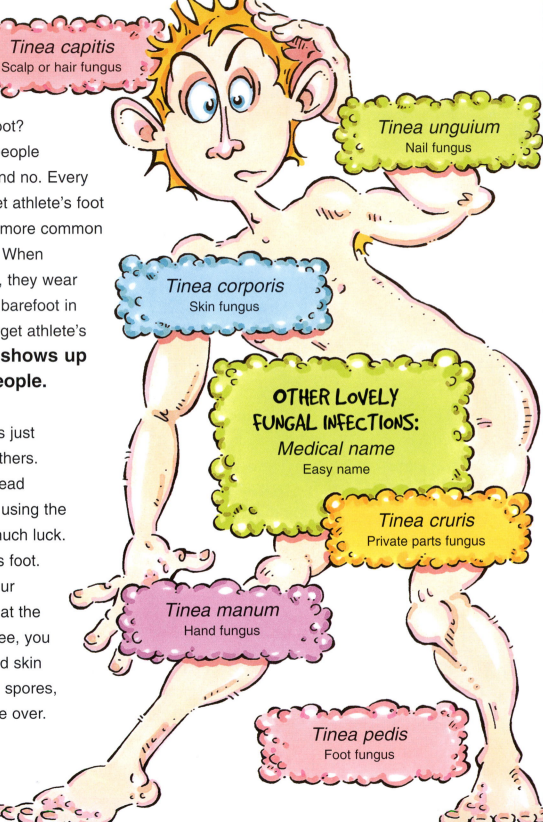

Tinea capitis
Scalp or hair fungus

Tinea unguium
Nail fungus

Tinea corporis
Skin fungus

OTHER LOVELY FUNGAL INFECTIONS:
Medical name
Easy name

Tinea cruris
Private parts fungus

Tinea manum
Hand fungus

Tinea pedis
Foot fungus

There is no simple way to tell if the fungus loves you. If it does, you will get foot ringworm. If it doesn't, your tootsies will never experience *tinea pedis.*

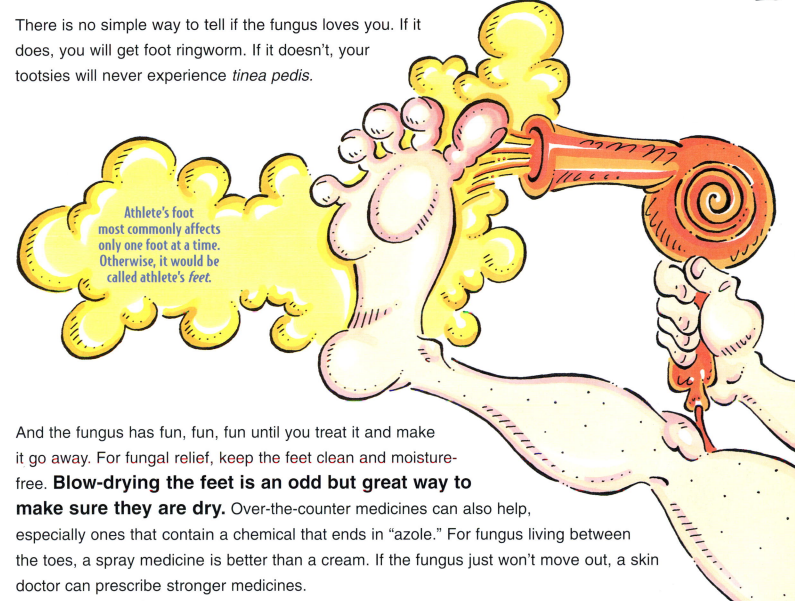

Athlete's foot most commonly affects only one foot at a time. Otherwise, it would be called athlete's *feet.*

And the fungus has fun, fun, fun until you treat it and make it go away. For fungal relief, keep the feet clean and moisture-free. **Blow-drying the feet is an odd but great way to make sure they are dry.** Over-the-counter medicines can also help, especially ones that contain a chemical that ends in "azole." For fungus living between the toes, a spray medicine is better than a cream. If the fungus just won't move out, a skin doctor can prescribe stronger medicines.

Not getting athlete's foot is easy. Keep your feet clean and dry. Maybe even powder them after a bath. Wear cotton or wool socks. Don't wear the same shoes every day or wear breathable shoes. Don't share towels or shoes. Wear flip-flops or sandals in public showers and swimming pools. If you really want to grow a family of *tinea pedis,* do just the opposite.

BRAINS

Brain surgery has been around for a long time.

Stone Age people chipped or hacked small holes into the skulls of their living friends. Maybe it was to relieve the pressure of a really bad headache. Or maybe it was to release evil spirits. In the Middle Ages, **skull drilling** was still practiced. Only then they used metal tools. When you think about it, drilling for brains made sense. Your head hurts, find the part that aches and get rid of it. There weren't many painkillers for the patients. That is partly okay because the brain itself does not feel pain. Brain, no pain. However, the skull and the hair feel a whole lot of pain. Just think of how it hurts when the class bully pulls your hair. Brain surgery has come a long way.

Brains look like your intestines made into a gelatin mold.

There is nothing quite like a brain. Brains look like a giant gray cauliflower on a very thin stalk or like half of a peeled orange. Slice a piece of brain and it looks like strudel—brain strudel.

If you have had the rare opportunity to hold a human brain, you would notice that it is **firm and spongy,** not really squishy and mushy. If you mixed Jell-O and pudding, you would have the texture of a brain. Pickled brains that you can touch are older and harder than a live human brain. Your human brain is alive right now. No kidding! Your brain is floating on the end of a thin stem in its very protective case called the bony cap, or skull. It is ¼ inch thick on top and thicker at the base. It is tough stuff, but that doesn't mean you should forget your helmet when you ride your bike. Brain splattered on the sidewalk is not a pretty sight. The skull does what it can, but really hard things like cement and metal can crush it.

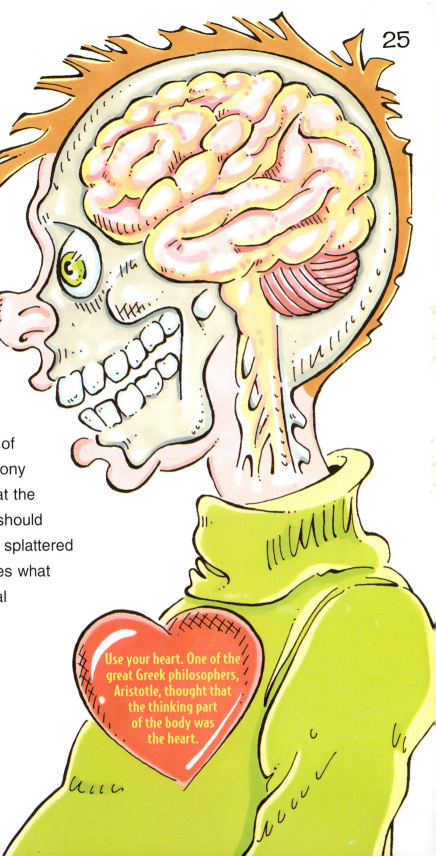

Use your heart. One of the great Greek philosophers, Aristotle, thought that the thinking part of the body was the heart.

A bruised brain is called a cerebral contusion.

Even without hitting the sidewalk, your brain gets slammed around all of the time. When you sit up in bed, your brain gets crammed against the back of your skull. Just imagine a poor brain during a roller coaster ride. The brains of boxers who died after a long punching career look kind of like old guacamole.

Actually, the brain doesn't get scraped or bruised easily because it is wrapped in three thin, strong bags. The brain bags are named the **dura mater**, the **pia mater**, and the **arachnoid mater**

The Nina, the Pinta and the Santa Maria. Anyway, *mater* means "mother" in Latin. How sweet. *Dura* means tough. So, the first sack is a tough mother. *Arachnoid* means "spiderlike" and this sack looks like a cobweb. *Pia* means "gentle." The innermost sack is very fragile.

Between the spider-mother sack and the gentle-mother sack is a liquid that acts as a brain shock absorber. The cerebrospinal fluid, or CSF, is like a travelling headrest. About half a glass of CSF drips into your brain every day. The clear, watery liquid contains proteins, salts, sugar, and urea. Urea is the same stuff that's found in pee pee. And your brain floats around in it.

The bags, the fluid, and the box are the wrappings around the precious jewel—the brain. That ugly, bumpy, three-pound mass is 85% water. Still, without it, nothing would work. **You actually feel with your brain, hear with your brain, and taste with your brain.** Your brain creates moods and memories. Without a brain you are like a vegetable. Well, actually worse, you are dead. Your brain is the control center. It is not a very good-looking control center—gray on the outside, white on the inside, and a wormlike surface. But the 30 billion nerve cells inside constantly fire electrochemcial messages. In each second, your brain is capable of sending more messages than the postal service does in your whole lifetime. So, who cares if it is ugly?

Those Egyptian mummies in museums are all brainless.
To help preserve the bodies, the brains were removed.
They used long hooks to pull each part of
the brain out through the nose.

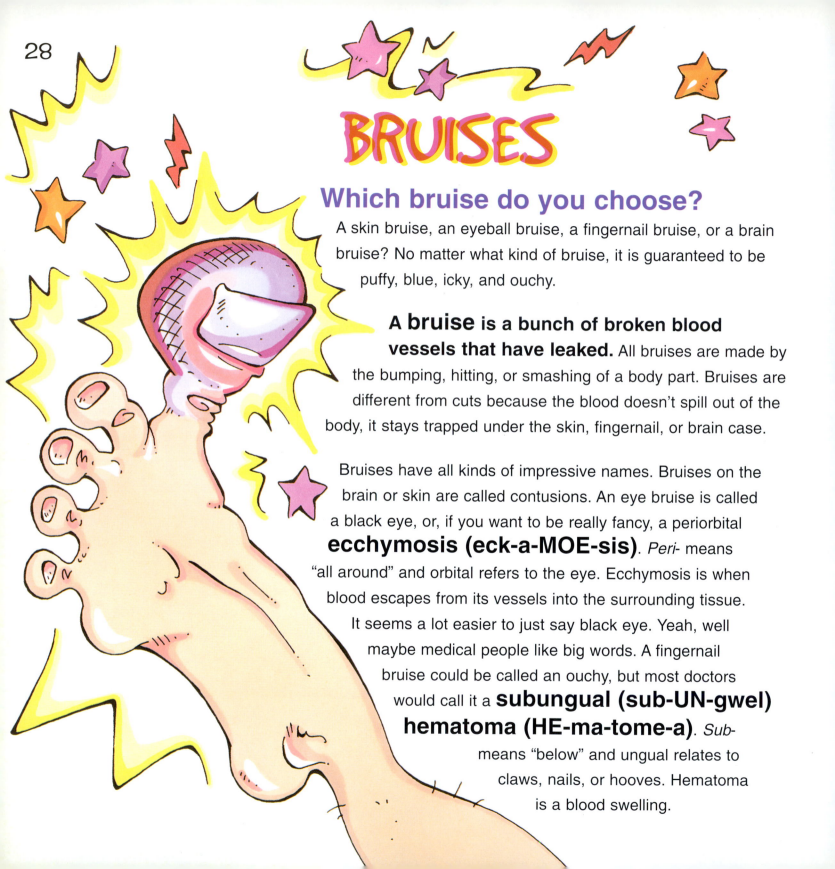

BRUISES

Which bruise do you choose?

A skin bruise, an eyeball bruise, a fingernail bruise, or a brain bruise? No matter what kind of bruise, it is guaranteed to be puffy, blue, icky, and ouchy.

A bruise is a bunch of broken blood vessels that have leaked. All bruises are made by the bumping, hitting, or smashing of a body part. Bruises are different from cuts because the blood doesn't spill out of the body, it stays trapped under the skin, fingernail, or brain case.

Bruises have all kinds of impressive names. Bruises on the brain or skin are called contusions. An eye bruise is called a black eye, or, if you want to be really fancy, a periorbital **ecchymosis (eck-a-MOE-sis)**. *Peri-* means "all around" and orbital refers to the eye. Ecchymosis is when blood escapes from its vessels into the surrounding tissue. It seems a lot easier to just say black eye. Yeah, well maybe medical people like big words. A fingernail bruise could be called an ouchy, but most doctors would call it a **subungual (sub-UN-gwel) hematoma (HE-ma-tome-a)**. *Sub-* means "below" and ungual relates to claws, nails, or hooves. Hematoma is a blood swelling.

So, it is a blood swelling under a fingernail. Enough with the big words. No matter what you call them, bruises are not something you would want to order everyday.

"I would like a vanilla shake and a bruise to go, please."

Brain bruises are not very high on the list of choice bruises. Although you can't see a disgusting brain contusion, it can be very dangerous. If a person's brain gets slammed against the skull really hard, it can bruise.

Ouch!

The first of the three brain sacks rips open. The blood oozes out of the brain and into the second sack. It would be like wrapping pudding into three bags and the bag closest to the pudding tears open. So, the goopy pudding drools out and gets trapped in the second bag. What's scary is that a drooling brain causes a person to pass out and maybe lose consciousness for a long time. Most people are lucky enough to not get brain bruises.

Cartoon characters often put a steak on their eyes to heal a black eye. Actually, this used to be a common practice about fifty years ago. It turns out that the steak doesn't do anything special. It is just cold. So, an ice pack would work just as well, though it wouldn't be as tasty.

Skin bruises are very common. You probably get several every year. Your skin is the largest organ of your body. Its job is to protect you. However, humans are clumsy so they often bump into things or things bump into them.

"Hey, that couch jumped right in front of me!"

A patch of skin about as big as a postage stamp is packed with about three feet of teeny tiny blood vessels. If these vessels get smushed, they will break open and drip out blood into the lower layers of skin. The top layer of skin has no blood vessels at all. It keeps the blood from seeping out. If the great red stuff actually drips out, it is not a bruise. It is a cut. Sometimes a wound can be surrounded by bruises.

Bruises are a very colorful event. A Technicolor bruise movie would start out in red, then turn blue and purple, and finish up with yellow and green. The lovely bruise may also have a glossy finish, due to fluids collecting in the area to make the skin stretch. Your body is not very fond of bruises. It sends in the white blood cell troops to get rid of the mess. The white blood cells clean out the trashed blood. As they do their job, the bruise changes color. In a couple of weeks, their job is complete. They leave no sign that a Technicolor bruise event has just taken place. Good little white blood cells.

Some people find the Technicolor bruise show to be rather disgusting. These people are not interested in observing great special effects. Lucky for them, the entire bruise show can be shortened.

To speed up the healing process, you can place ice packs or even a bag of frozen vegetables on the bruise right away for the first day. After the first day, apply heat.

Vitamin K cream or arnica cream may also help the bruise to disappear more quickly. Also, bruises tend to heal more slowly the lower they are on the body. A leg bruise will heal more slowly than an arm bruise. Immediately wrapping a leg bruise in an elastic bandage will stop the bleeding more quickly, so the bruise will not be as nasty.

Some people think that black eyes are the best bruises since they make you look tough. Other people think that black eyes are the worst bruises because they make you look weird.

A periorbital ecchymosis is nothing more than a regular bruise, but in a bad spot.

The eye itself doesn't actually get purple and blue, just the skin around the eye. Sometimes little vessels in the eye may break and turn the eye bloody. Fists, elbows, and falls are the most common causes of a black eye. If you get hit in the nose, you can get a black eye. If you barf too much, you can get a black eye. No, it is not from the force of the vomit hitting you in the eye.

Smash your finger with a hammer and you don't get a black eye. You get a fingernail bruise. A slamming car door is another great way to get this bruise. The fingernail itself doesn't actually get bruised; it is the nailbed under the fingernail that oozes blood.

Cringe, cringe.

The problem with this bruise is pressure. With pressure comes pain. Oh, the pain. Your little pinkie can become the only thing you think about. The answer— relieve the pain. That is, if you can take the cure. A doctor can pierce the nail with the tip of a red hot needle. A little hole is burned through the nail and the blood spurts out.

Ahhhh, relief!

Caution flammable! Fingernail bruises under fake nails cannot be cured in this manner without the risk of setting them on fire.

EYEBALLS

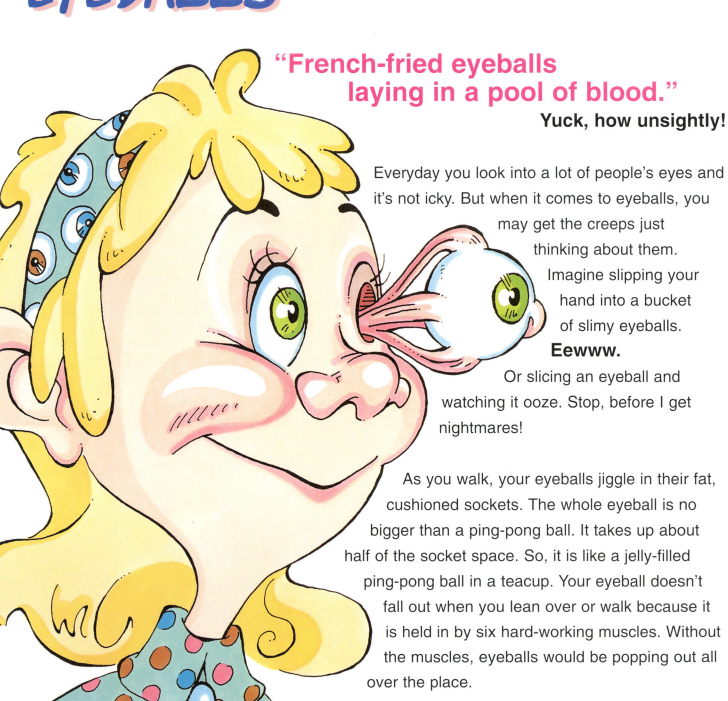

"French-fried eyeballs laying in a pool of blood."

Yuck, how unsightly!

Everyday you look into a lot of people's eyes and it's not icky. But when it comes to eyeballs, you may get the creeps just thinking about them. Imagine slipping your hand into a bucket of slimy eyeballs. **Eewww.** Or slicing an eyeball and watching it ooze. Stop, before I get nightmares!

As you walk, your eyeballs jiggle in their fat, cushioned sockets. The whole eyeball is no bigger than a ping-pong ball. It takes up about half of the socket space. So, it is like a jelly-filled ping-pong ball in a teacup. Your eyeball doesn't fall out when you lean over or walk because it is held in by six hard-working muscles. Without the muscles, eyeballs would be popping out all over the place.

The muscles also pull your eyeball back and forth, so you can read and look around. Watch your baby-sitter's eyeballs while reading this book. The eyeballs don't move along smoothly. They jerk along like a fish caught on a line. The eyeball muscles yank, heave, and tug at the eyes to move them along. **Each day these muscles move about 100,000 times.** For your leg muscles to get the same workout, you would have to walk about 50 miles.

What is better than getting poked in the eye with a sharp stick? Most *anything* is better than getting poked in the eye with a sharp stick. Your eyes are protected—nestled in a hole with a forehead roof and cheekbone floor.

In 1793, a French girl was born with one eye in the center of her forehead. Her one eye worked just fine for fifteen years until she died.

ODD EYEBALL SAYINGS
the saying followed by what it means:

"My eye" – Nonsense
"Keep your eye on the ball" – Be alert
"Keep your eyes peeled" – Be extremely alert
"Pull the wool over your eyes" – To fool someone
"Sight for sore eyes" – Something that gives pleasure
"Red-eye special" – Travel in the middle of the night
"An eye for an eye" – Tit for tat
"Apple of my eye" – My darling
"Deadeye" – Sure shot
"Evil eye" – Bad luck
"Twinkle of an eye" – Very quickly
"Stink eye" – Dirty looks

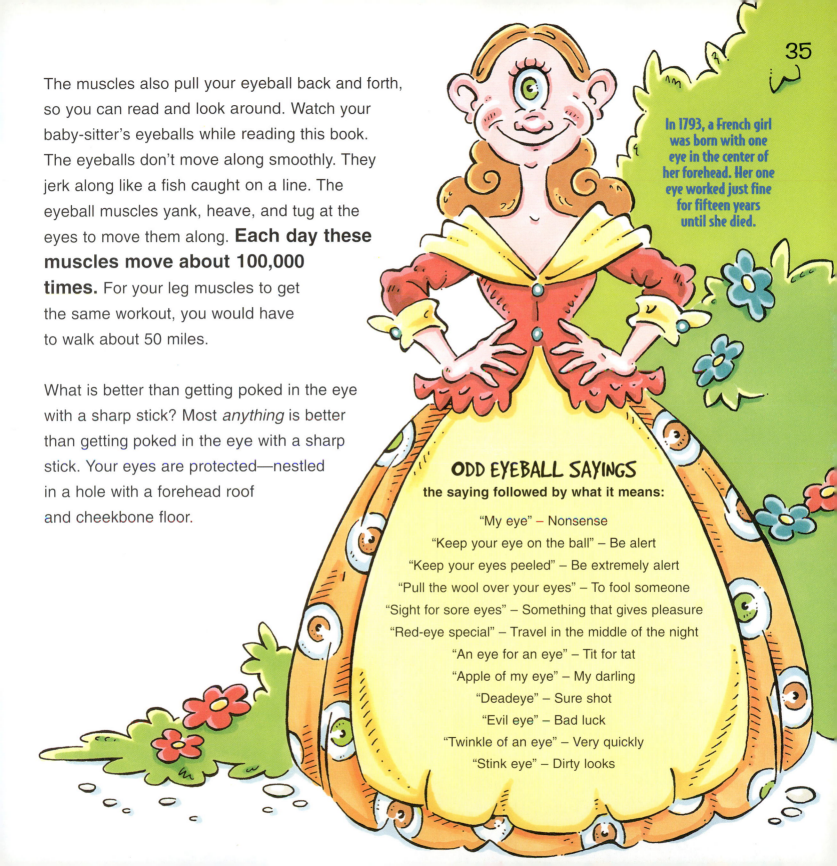

In 1895, an English company announced it would make X-ray glasses. The glasses never happened but a London department store made a bunch of money selling "X-ray proof" underwear.

EYE DISSECTION

What you need:

A pair of scissors, a single-edged razor blade, a cow or sheep eyeball (these are available from butcher shops or from a science supply house), a newspaper, and permission.

What you do:

Ask your parents if it is okay for you to do this experiment. If it is all right, obtain an eyeball.

Place the eyeball on a sheet of newspaper. Get used to it staring back at you. Turn the eyeball over and locate the optic nerve. Notice the muscles that attach to the eyeball. Using the scissors, cut away the tissue from the eyeball.

Cut the eyeball in half by piercing the wall of the eyeball and cutting all the way around. Lift off the back half. Place the front half back into staring position. Use the razor blade to cut along the outer edge of the cornea. Lift off the cornea. The aqueous humor will seep out. The iris, or color part of the eye, should be left. Look through the iris opening, or pupil, to find the lens. Carefully cut around the lens to remove it.

Place the lens on the newspaper. What do you notice?

Clean up your eyeball mess.

You may want to play around with the lens for awhile.

A tough fibrous case, called the sclera (SCLEAR-a), covers the eyeball. This is the "white of the eye." **"Don't fire until you see the whites of their eyes."**

The clear, tough coating over the colored part of the eye is called the cornea (CORN-knee-a). Your eyelid also protects your eye. Throw a wadded sheet of paper at your best friend. His or her eyelids will close. "We will protect you, eyeball!" If all of the protection failed and you got poked in the eye with a sharp stick, it would be very gooey. Beneath the white eye case is a bunch of jelly called the **vitreous (VIT-ree-us) humor**.

What's so funny about it? Not humor as in ha-ha but *humor* as in the Latin word for **moisture**. The fluid is similar to thick egg whites. The vitreous humor stops the eyeball from collapsing like the water in a punctured water balloon. A collapsing eyeball would be a very nasty thing.

"Look into my eyes. Deep into my eyes."

What are you seeing when you do look into someone's eyes? The front window is the cornea. It is actually a tiny bulge on the smooth eyeball. Doctors shave off layers of the cornea with lasers to correct eyesight. **"Here let me just carve off a little of your eyeball."** The cornea bends light as it comes into your eye. Changing the way the light bends will make objects clearer.

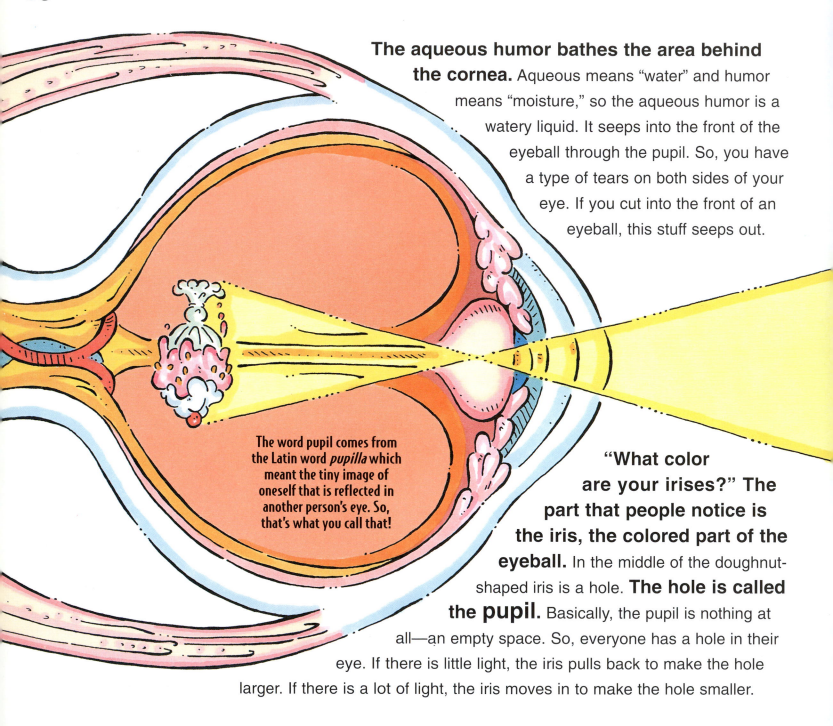

The aqueous humor bathes the area behind the cornea. Aqueous means "water" and humor means "moisture," so the aqueous humor is a watery liquid. It seeps into the front of the eyeball through the pupil. So, you have a type of tears on both sides of your eye. If you cut into the front of an eyeball, this stuff seeps out.

The word pupil comes from the Latin word *pupilla* which meant the tiny image of oneself that is reflected in another person's eye. So, that's what you call that!

"What color are your irises?" The part that people notice is the iris, the colored part of the eyeball. In the middle of the doughnut-shaped iris is a hole. **The hole is called the pupil.** Basically, the pupil is nothing at all—an empty space. So, everyone has a hole in their eye. If there is little light, the iris pulls back to make the hole larger. If there is a lot of light, the iris moves in to make the hole smaller.

If you had a teensy lightbulb inside of your eyeball, the light would shine out through your pupil. Whoa! The pupil is a keyhole into your eyeball. Medical people use a special instrument with a light and lenses to peek into the area behind the hole in your eyeball.

The pupil opens to the lens. Think of M&M's™ candy that has been left in the sun for a short time. (No, not the peanut kind.) The sides are soft and the middle is still firm. The lens is similar. Unlike the candy, the lens is flexible. Tiny muscles make it fatter to see close and flatter to see far. **The lens is used for the fine focus, while the main focus is in the cornea.** Behind the lens is the eye gelatin and the back wall. And that's it!

But how does the eye work? Since you insist, here goes. Light bounces off of an object. The cornea bends the light rays and sends them through the pupil. Then the lens does some fine tuning, the light goes through the gelatin in the eyeball, and lands on the back wall where a little upside down image is formed. The back wall transmits the message through the optic nerve, to the brain, two thousandths of a second later, where the brain sorts it all out.

Belladonna—what a beautiful name. Deadly nightshade is another name for this poisonous, not so beautiful herb. Put a drop of the sap in your eye. No? That is what women did during the Italian Renaissance to enlarge the pupils of their eyes.

GUTS

"I hate your guts!"

**Actually, you would probably
hate *everyone's* guts
                 since they are very disgusting.**

"It was a gut instinct."
Guts definitely are not the thinking or feeling part of
the body. "I puked my guts out." Sooo, not possible.
"He's got a lot of guts." Yeah, so does everyone else.
"Let's get to the gut of the matter."

What are guts anyway?

If you watch a movie and a person's guts are hanging out,
what are they holding? If you gut an animal, what part do
you remove? Guts are the entrails. Guts are the bowels.
**Basically, guts are the stomach
                 and the intestines.**

So, when someone has a lot of guts, you are really saying
they have a lot of intestines and stomach. If you have a gut
instinct, does that mean your stomach is talking to you?

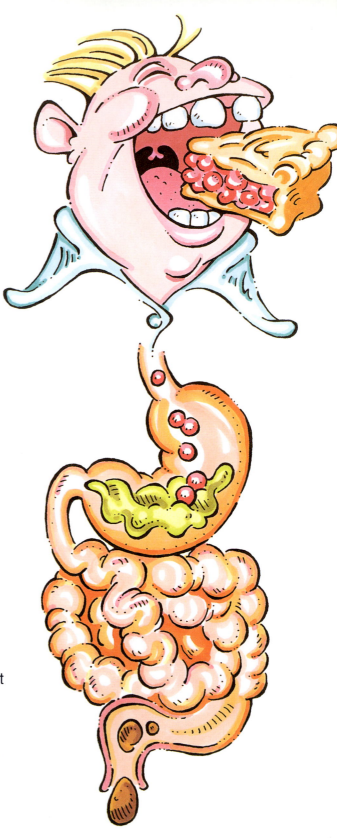

Your stomach is a J-shaped sack that rests right above your belly button area. Your gut tubes wind around and around beneath your belly button area. Unwind them and you could stretch them across a tennis court. Hey, who needs a net?

The first twenty feet of gut tube is **the small intestine**. The last five is the **large intestine.**

The small intestine is called that because the tube is smaller than the large intestine. How clever! It is about the size of a Polish sausage. The small intestine is nice and smooth on the outside and like a skin shag rug on the inside. At the entrance, the stomach dumps mushed up food that looks like barf.

Actually, it is barf if it comes back up and exits out your mouth. If it stays where it belongs, in your guts, it is called **chyme (KIME).**

Alexis St. Martin became a living laboratory after he was accidentally shot in the stomach. The wound healed but a hole in the stomach remained.
Dr. William Beaumont used the hole as a window into the stomach. Beaumont put different foods into the hole and then pulled them out to see what had happened to them.

After the small intestine does its job of sucking out the nutrients from chyme, it squeezes it out the end into the large intestine.

Think of a long chain of hollow fists. That is about how your large intestine looks—a string of lumps smooth inside and out. The last eight inches is the rectum, where poo is stored before it goes out the anus exit door. **The whole job of the large gut tube, or colon, is to suck water out of the used-up meal turning what you've eaten into poop**. If you had a liter bottle of this pre-poop material, the large intestine would suck out a small juice can full of water during this process. After the chyme sits in your colon for three to ten hours, enough water has been sucked out for it to officially become caca. Poops hang out in the last section of the tube until it is shoved into the rectum and out into the world. "Good-bye, warm colon. Hello, cold cruel world."

To move all of the crappy stuff around, your guts pinch and shove, pinch and shove all the way down the line. It is kind of like squeezing a toothpaste tube. Mostly you don't feel it unless you have occasional diarrhea or constant irritable bowel syndrome. Yep, angry guts are not a pleasant experience. Your guts pinch. Ouch! Cramp! And shove! Whoa! Toilet quick! Needless to say, people with irritable bowel syndrome are just that—irritable.

Guts are held in by skin, layers of fat, and abs, or abdominal muscles. Remove these layers and the guts will fall out. Sometimes this could be good—especially if you like to eat guts. Chitlins are cooked pig intestines. Haggis is stuffed sheep stomachs. The tubes that sausage is stuffed into? Intestines. But don't worry, all of the pre-poop stuff and the poo is cleaned out before serving.

GUT MUSIC

Most people fart about 14 times every day—sometimes more, sometimes less. A fart is gas escaping from your anus. The gas comes from bacteria breaking down food in your intestine.

A **flatograph** keeps track of the number of toots in a single day.

When you conduct the following experiment, keep in mind that each fart must be separated by several seconds. A series of tiny toots will count as one fart.

What you need: Six sheets of paper, pencil, ruler, yourself.

What you do:

Make a **FLATOGRAPH**. The horizontal line represents the number of days that you will conduct the experiment—write in the 5 days you'll be conducting the experiment. The vertical line represents the number of times that you fart each day—add in the numbers 1 through 25.

Begin the experiment first thing in the morning, and be sure to have a sheet of paper and a pencil on hand. Write Day One at the top of the paper. Each time you fart, make a slash on the paper. This is your Fart Tally Sheet. Also record on the tally sheet the food you eat throughout the day. At the close of the day, total the number of farts on your sheet. On your Flatograph, locate the number that corresponds to your fart total. Draw a line up from your Day One mark to your fart number. You can make the line into a box and color it in if you want. Continue tallying your farts and writing down your food for four more days. Are you more gaseous on some days than others?

Sometimes it isn't your tummy that you hear rumbling, it is your intestines. Gurgling sounds in the intestines are called borborygmi. The gut opera is presented by gas moving through the gut tubes.

CONSTIPATION

Sometimes you just can't go.

Maybe you're upset, maybe you held it for too long, maybe you don't like to use an alien bathroom, maybe you haven't been eating right, maybe you're taking medicine. Whatever the reason, you are stopped-up or constipated.

So, what do you do? **Most people whine, "I can't go."** And it's okay to whine because **constipation (con-sta-PAY-shun)** is not very fun. Some people buy laxatives at the drugstore. These laxatives force the gut to pinch and cramp. About eight hours later, they poop. That is not okay because taking gut stimulant laxatives can make it so you can't dookie without using them.

Ever notice ads on the TV for constipation cures? The next time you see this type of ad on TV pay close attention. Would you be smiling like the person in the advertisement if you had this probelm?

Other people insert tubes into their buttholes and squirt water or salty water into their rectum. **This is called an enema (EN-a-ma).** About three to five minutes later, they poop. Although they are a bit messy, enemas aren't dangerous. The problem is if you take too many enemas, you can't poop on your own.

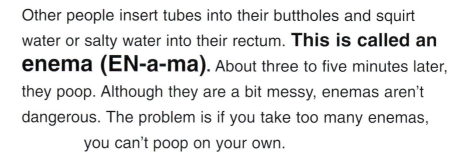

Lots of fiber or bulk is the cure of choice for many stopped-up people. They eat prunes, bran, raw vegetables, and raw fruit. Or they buy fiber supplements or stool softeners from the store. Bulk producers and stool-softening laxatives are OK to use because they don't force your gut muscles to push and shove the poo out. Instead they help by adding moisture to the poops to make them easier to get out. One or two days later, they deliver poop. This is probably the safest thing to do. For most people, patience is the answer. Usually the poop will pass if the "Oh no! I didn't go today!" person relaxes and waits.

A diet with a lot of cookies and sodas and other refined foods is one avoidable cause of this rear end problem. When food is digested, it collects in the last part of the colon, or the end of the large intestine.

**Here the body usually stores poop,
or feces (FEE-cees),
until you let it go in the toilet.**

If the poop doesn't have a lot of fiber or bulk, it stays in the colon. Water continues to draw away since the doo doo stays in the colon longer than usual. The poop becomes compact and hard instead of squishy and soft. At the toilet, the hardened turd doesn't come out easily. The rectum has to push and strain to get the poop out. To avoid constipation all you need to do is eat fresh vegetables, fruits, and bran. Also drink lots of water everyday.

Being too busy to answer the call of nature is another friend of constipation. Again the poop stays in the colon and gets hard. Then when the too-busy-to-poop person tries to relieve themselves, it won't come out. So, poop regularly; don't hold it.

"Yuck! I hate castor oil." In the olden days, mothers lovingly forced teaspoons of castor oil down the throats of their children to keep their bowel movements regular. And you complain about having to eat your vegetables!

A really, really, really, really bad case of constipation can cause **fecal impaction**. Fecal means "poop" and impaction means that it becomes firmly stuck because of pressing. A fecal impaction is NOT something you want to request for your birthday. Nurses and doctors get the lovely job of removing a fecal impaction. Sometimes the patient's butt is put to sleep with medication. The doctor then goes into the rectum, breaks up the stuck poop, and pulls it out. I'm sure both the doctor and the patient are relieved when the whole thing is over.

Not being regular is different for everybody. Some people dookie two times a day; some people poop less often. So, the next time your poo patterns are irregular, remember it's okay if you don't poop every day. Drink water, eat fiber, and relax. This too shall pass.

GOOSE BUMPS

What does a plucked goose look like?

This all-important, life-altering question can be easily answered. Take a look at your own skin the next time you get frightened or chilly. That is what the skin of a plucked goose looks like. **Thus, the name "goose bumps," or "goose pimples," or "gooseflesh."**

Take a very close look at your arm. Right now? Yes, immediately. Notice that you are actually very hairy. Humans used to have a lot more hair. Even more hair than your Uncle Fred. Through time, humans lost much of their hair covering. However, fine little hairs still cover most of your body.

No one knows for certain why goose bumps are called goose bumps and not chicken bumps, duck bumps, or turkey bumps.

Each hair on your body grows from an opening called a follicle (FOLL-ick-ul).

Hairs also have special muscles called *arrector pili* that go from deep in the skin to the hair follicles. The *arrector pili* act as an erector to raise the hair from its resting position on your skin.

If you have ever observed a chilly dove or a cold kitten, the animal will puff up its feathers or fur. The trapped air is warmed by body heat and it creates a warm blanket surrounding the animal. Humans do the same thing. When you get cold, the muscles at the bottom of each follicle quickly contract, raising your body hair to help you warm up. The problem is that humans no longer have fur. The follicles don't know this, so they still contract to erect the hairs. The skin around each hair makes a bump to support the hair. But, the mostly hairless skin doesn't have the same effect.

Shivering is a good way to keep warm. The shivers are actually muscles contracting. The working muscles give off heat that helps to warm you up.

The result is bumps. Goose bumps!

Getting gooseflesh from fear could be a response to the "cold sweat" that automatically breaks out when a person becomes startled. You cannot control this sweat. The body is not releasing the sweat to cool down. Instead, the body produces a quick response to warm it back up again. Goose bumps!

When dogs, cats, or bears become frightened, they ruffle up their fur. This makes the animal look bigger and tougher. "Don't mess with me. I'm big and tough." When fearful, humans may break out in goose pimples for the same reason. Since humans no longer have lots of hair, they just look silly, not tough.

So, do geese get goose bumps? Actually, under their feathers they probably do. However, if you can't see them, are they really goose pimples?

Even a completely bald man will feel his hair stand on end from sudden terror. Okay, so it is not actually hair but a prickly sensation on his head.

HICCUPS

Hiccup. . .   Hiccup. . .   Hiccup. . .   **BOO!**

Hiccup.

Humans have hiccuped throughout the ages. Cave people probably got the occasional attack. Even fetuses in the womb get hiccups. Or is it hiccough? Some medical people insist on calling them hiccoughs. But the noise itself sounds more like hick up. Okay, the "hic" in a hiccup is caused by air sucking into your lungs.

The "cup" sound is made by a special little flap called the epiglottis (epp-a-GLOT-us) slamming closed over your windpipe.

Hic—swoosh, cup—slam. These annoying and sometimes entertaining little oddities are actually difficult for your body to make.

This minor event takes a whole lot of coordination inside your body. Hiccoughs, sorry, hiccups occur when a muscle barrier between your stomach and lungs called the **diaphragm (DIE-a-fram)** goes spastic.

The diaphragm is all-important for breathing. Breathe in. The diaphragm drops down to make a lung vacuum, so air sucks in. Breathe out. The diaphragm relaxes, goes up, and shoves the air out. Usually, the diaphragm has pretty good control. But sometimes it gets irritated and the rhythm is thrown off. Sometimes instead of hiccuping, you just hic, hic, hic. When that happens, the diaphragm is going through spasms.

No one is quite sure why the diaphragm becomes so irritated. It could be from eating too much, so the puffed up stomach presses on the wall of muscle. Or too much air being sucked in affects the regular breathing pattern. Or lifting something incorrectly tweaks the diaphragm. What is known is that almost everyone at some point upsets the diaphragm into hiccuping.

One day, when he was 26 years old, George Osborn, an Iowa farmer, tried to lift a 350 pound hog. He started to hiccup. The farmer hiccuped through two marriages and eight children until his death 69 years later. He lived a normal life, except it was hard to keep in his false teeth.

52

HICCUP CURES THAT DON'T ACTUALLY WORK:

Hold your breath for one minute.

Swallow a teaspoon of sugar.

Drink a glass of water slowly.

Drink water from the opposite side of the cup.

Have someone surprise you. "Boo!"

Breathe into a paper bag.

Give a forceful yank to your tongue. "Ouch!"

Chew and swallow dry bread.

Pull your knees up to your chest or lean forward.

Don't think about your hiccups.

Cover your head with a wastebasket and have someone beat on it.

Spit on a rock and then turn it over.

Wet a piece of red thread with your tongue, hang the thread from your forehead, look at the thread.

Suck on a slice of lemon.

Go for a walk in the sunshine.

In 1768, an Englishman was admitted to the hospital with hiccups. His hiccups were so loud they could be heard a half-mile away.

So much for the hic. What about the cup part? The cup part happens up in your throat. **At the end of your tongue and right before your vocal chords is the epiglottis.** This little flap has a very serious job. It protects your windpipe from unwanted stuff like food. When you breathe, the epiglottis keeps the windpipe open. But when you swallow, the epiglottis shuts over the air pipe and reroutes the food down the food tube.

"Food on the way. Batten down the hatches."

Sometimes the epiglottis gets a little confused, especially if you talk or laugh with your mouth full.

You go: **"Blah, gulp, blah, ha, ha, gulp, gulp, blah."**

Your epiglottis goes: **"Open, close, open, open, open, close, close, open?"**

You go: **Choke, choke, choke. Cough, cough.**

Food hitting the opening of the windpipe causes an alert to expel rushes of air to push the invader out.

And back to the cup part? The cup part. Yes, the cup part happens when the epiglottis frantically snaps the windpipe closed to stop the rush of air. Usually, you don't hear the epiglottis shutting. However, in this case it is slamming closed over the opening and it is halting a big swoosh of air. Cup, cup, cup. Nope, you can't have that happen. The cup always follows the hic. Nor can you have cuphic, cuphic. It is and forever will be hiccup.

The sure cure for hiccups doesn't exist. They go away in due time. However, humans have created a whole bunch of remedies. Hospitals may give hiccupers drugs to deaden the nerve that causes the diaphragm to contract. However, most of us just hiccup away until they go away. Hiccup, **hiccup. Gone.**

KNUCKLE CRACKING

The toe bone's connected to the foot bone. Crack.

The foot bone's connected to the leg bone. **Crack.**

The leg bone's connected to the knee bone. **Crack.**

The finger bone's connected to the finger bone.

Crack, crack, crack.

"Stop cracking your knuckles. That's so vile."
Vile? Yes, vile is a fancy word for disgusting.

For the person doing the cracking it is, "Ahhhhh, relief." For the person listening to the cracker it is, "Euuuuwww. Stop already." Popping your knuckles isn't all that it is cracked up to be. Ha, ha very punny. You actually don't crack anything at all. The bones don't break, nor does the knuckle. The bones are not grinding together. What you are doing is pressurizing and displacing the liquid inside the knuckle. Huh?

About 1 out of 4 people are knuckle crackers.

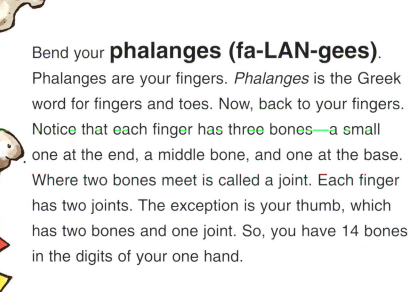

Bend your **phalanges (fa-LAN-gees)**. Phalanges are your fingers. *Phalanges* is the Greek word for fingers and toes. Now, back to your fingers. Notice that each finger has three bones—a small one at the end, a middle bone, and one at the base. Where two bones meet is called a joint. Each finger has two joints. The exception is your thumb, which has two bones and one joint. So, you have 14 bones in the digits of your one hand.

The bones are held together by straps of tissue called ligaments. Ligaments can hold the bones very tight or they can be more loose. Maybe you have a classmate whose claim to fame is the weird things he can do with his finger. These special people are said to be double-jointed. What they really are is long-ligamented. No one has multiple joints. What they do have is especially long ligaments, which allow them to move their joints in very entertaining ways.

Some people can easily crack their knuckles. Others cannot perform this feat at all, no matter how much tugging.

Even though the ligaments connect the bones in your moveable joints, there is still some space between the joints. This space, or the joint cavity, is filled with fluid. The liquid coats the ends of the bones, nourishes the area, kills germs, and removes garbage collected from bone wear and tear. The light yellow fluid looks and feels like egg white. Also in the liquid are dissolved gases, such as the carbon dioxide that you breathe out. When the joint is still, the fluid is thick. But it thins out when the joint moves.

Finger tugging causes the two bones in a joint to pull apart. This creates a vacuum. If you have ever tried to pull up on a suction cup, you notice a vacuum has formed inside. The empty space makes the gas in the joint fluid change into bubbles. So, do the bubbles pop to make the noise?

Nope, more fluid crashes in, the joint snaps back and

CRACK!

After a satisfying pop, a knuckle will not crack again for 20 to 30 minutes. Go ahead and try. This is because leftover bubbles act like shock absorbers. It takes a few minutes for these bubbles to go back into solution to become part of the joint fluid once again. Some pops, creaks, and cracks are caused by tendons and ligaments snapping over a bone. Knees, ankles, and wrists are known for making this type of music. Ahhh, music to no one's ears. The next time your great auntie says, "Stop cracking your knuckles or you will get arthritis." You can tell her not to worry. **Knuckle popping does not lead to inflamed ("-itis") joints ("arthro-") later in life.** Although doctors are not completely sure what causes arthritis, knuckle cracking has been pretty much ruled out. On the other hand (ha-ha), a constant knuckle cracker has a weaker grip than people who don't crack their knuckles. You still may want to quiet your knuckle music around great auntie. Since it bothers her, she may not treat you to ice cream if you bug her too much.

TEN DONE TRICK

What you need:
You, your hand, and arm.

What you do:
Hold your hand out with your palm facing you.

Look at your wrist while you separately wiggle each finger.

See the wrist pulsing with your finger movements? And each finger causes a different spot to move. Amazing! How does it do that?!

The secret to this trick is tendons. Tendons are cords that connect your bones to your muscles. The tendons are why you can move your fingers to play a piano or pick your nose. Now, turn your hand over and do the same thing. See the tendons that go up the back of your hand?

MOLES

Cindy Crawford has one on her cheek. So beautiful. Marilyn Monroe was known for the one above her upper lip. How lovely. Some people paint them on, buy boxes of them to paste on, or even have them permanently placed on. In the French Court of the 1700s, they were very fashionable. All the rage. Moles? Moles. Aren't they beauty marks? Yes, beauty marks are just moles by a sweeter name.

Moles are skin spots. They are the most common growths on humans. Some people have less and some people have more. But almost everyone has 10 to 50 moles on their body. Count the moles on your body. They can be pink, light brown, dark brown, or black. Their shape may be round or oval. A mole may be a raised bump or flat. They can range in size from small to large areas. Moles can be cute like on a movie star or they can be huge, cauliflower bumps like on a witch's nose.

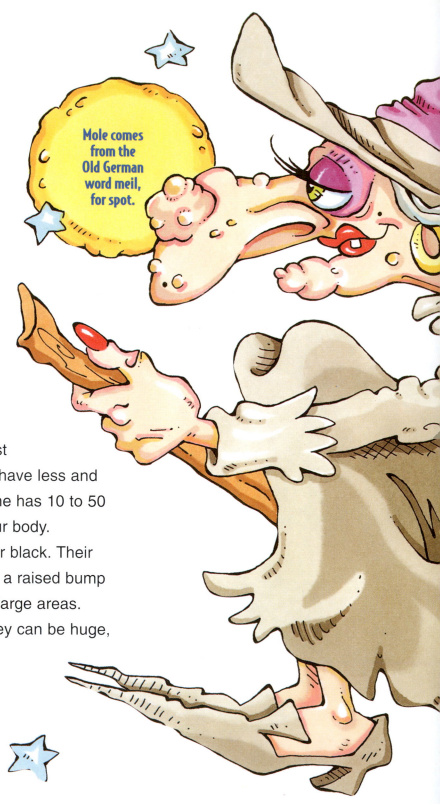

Mole comes from the Old German word meil, for spot.

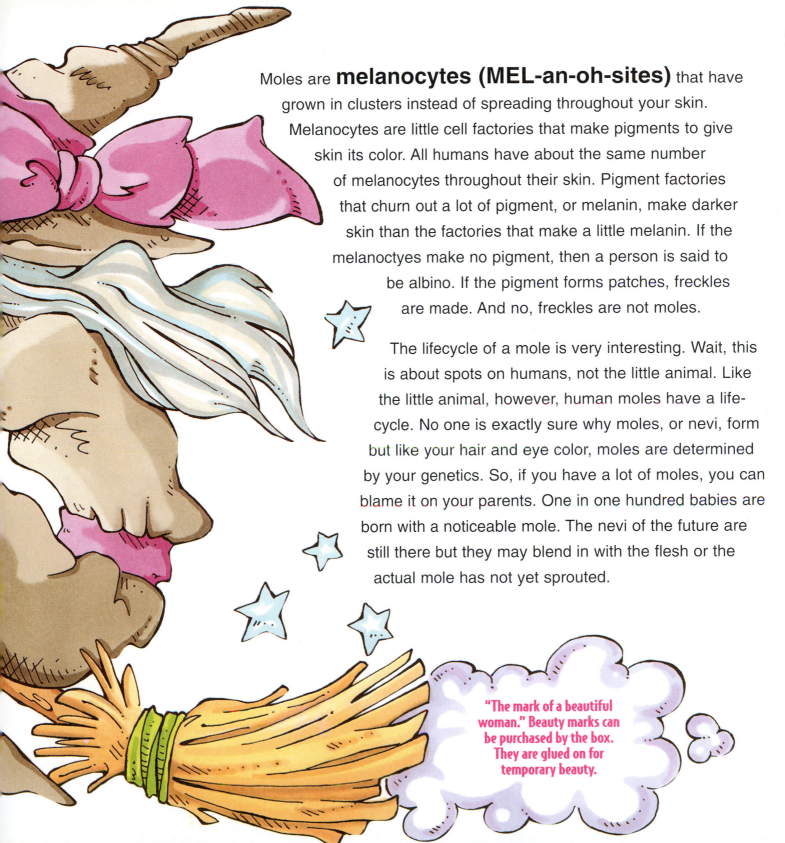

Moles are **melanocytes (MEL-an-oh-sites)** that have grown in clusters instead of spreading throughout your skin. Melanocytes are little cell factories that make pigments to give skin its color. All humans have about the same number of melanocytes throughout their skin. Pigment factories that churn out a lot of pigment, or melanin, make darker skin than the factories that make a little melanin. If the melanoctyes make no pigment, then a person is said to be albino. If the pigment forms patches, freckles are made. And no, freckles are not moles.

The lifecycle of a mole is very interesting. Wait, this is about spots on humans, not the little animal. Like the little animal, however, human moles have a life-cycle. No one is exactly sure why moles, or nevi, form but like your hair and eye color, moles are determined by your genetics. So, if you have a lot of moles, you can blame it on your parents. One in one hundred babies are born with a noticeable mole. The nevi of the future are still there but they may blend in with the flesh or the actual mole has not yet sprouted.

"The mark of a beautiful woman." Beauty marks can be purchased by the box. They are glued on for temporary beauty.

As you grow, your moles grow. In kids, they begin to show up as flat spots similar to freckles. As a teen, the base of the moles may rise. Whole new crops of moles may appear during the teen years. So, not only do you look forward to batches of pimples, you also get mole crops. Some may even sprout hairs. After hanging around for about 40 years, a mole may begin to pale. The aging mole may also protrude so much that it forms into a dome or a floppy ball. Usually, this old mole hangs on until the bitter end.

Since they will be around for a long time, you may want to become familiar with your nevi. Don't be surprised if a new one appears, since moles may show up at any time and any age. One man in his mid-forties developed dozens of moles over several months. He was not very happy about it. "Argh, the moles are invading!"

Some moles are bad. Very bad. About one mole in a million turns cancerous. These moles are not usually the little round ones but the atypical ones that are weird-shaped, odd-colored, or bumpy-surfaced. But even a normal mole sometimes becomes cancerous. A cancerous mole may lead to melanoma, a type of skin cancer. A doctor should examine suspicious moles. The doctor may remove the mole before it goes really bad.

Besides having moles removed for medical reasons, some people choose to have moles removed just because they don't like them. One person's beauty mark is another person's mole. Moles are dug out, electrocuted, frozen off, lasered away, burnt with acids, or chemically shrunk.

Olé! Away. Molé!

RASHES

All hives are rashes.
But not all rashes are hives.

Rashes can also be measles (itchy), chicken pox (scratchy), fever blisters (euwww), scalp ringworm (yuck), lice (ick), or **dermatitis (huh?)**. Derma- means "skin" and -titis means "inflamed." Like a volcano, sometimes your skin erupts. Unlike a volcano, you form red spots, patches, or blisters. These eruptions are rashes. The bumps itch, ooze, look disgusting, and make you unhappy.

EPIDERMIS

DERMIS

SUBCUTANEOUS

A whole lot of things can cause rashes to pop up, such as poisonous plants, viruses, fungus, allergies, even heat. Actually, just about anything that your body decides it doesn't like can cause rashes. "I don't like shellfish. Bring on a rash." "Cat hair, not for me. Rash time." Skin rashes are how your body tells you it is irritated. And when your body is irritated, you certainly know it. **Scratch, scratch.**

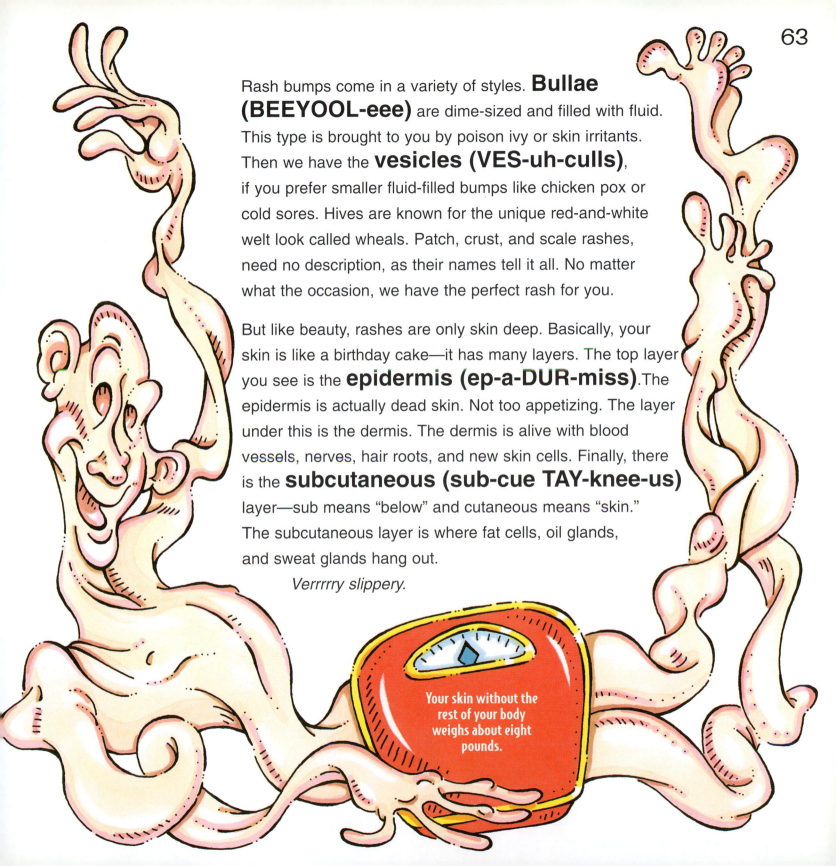

Rash bumps come in a variety of styles. **Bullae (BEEYOOL-eee)** are dime-sized and filled with fluid. This type is brought to you by poison ivy or skin irritants. Then we have the **vesicles (VES-uh-culls)**, if you prefer smaller fluid-filled bumps like chicken pox or cold sores. Hives are known for the unique red-and-white welt look called wheals. Patch, crust, and scale rashes, need no description, as their names tell it all. No matter what the occasion, we have the perfect rash for you.

But like beauty, rashes are only skin deep. Basically, your skin is like a birthday cake—it has many layers. The top layer you see is the **epidermis (ep-a-DUR-miss)**. The epidermis is actually dead skin. Not too appetizing. The layer under this is the dermis. The dermis is alive with blood vessels, nerves, hair roots, and new skin cells. Finally, there is the **subcutaneous (sub-cue TAY-knee-us)** layer—sub means "below" and cutaneous means "skin." The subcutaneous layer is where fat cells, oil glands, and sweat glands hang out.

Verrrrry slippery.

Your skin without the rest of your body weighs about eight pounds.

Depending upon your choice of rashes, they can form in different layers of your skin. Prickly heat is a top layer variety. Overheating makes sweat. Usually this is good, but if the sweat gets trapped under the surface, the skin cells get mad. "Go away. We don't like you." And when skin cells get irritated, they swell. Bump, bump, bump. Itch, itch, itch.

Hives are your body's way of telling you something's wrong: allergies. Some foods, medicines, dyes, detergents, animal hair, soaps, perfumes, and poison ivy just don't agree with everyone. The very handy skin tries to help out. "Don't worry. The skin to the rescue!"

Histamines (HISS-ta-means) flow and widen the blood vessels under your skin. The great fighting white blood cells rush in. Red and white welts pop up from the skin attack. You itch and burn and whine. Hey, your skin was only trying to help.

Stop,

don't touch your poison ivy blisters or the gunk inside will ooze and make the rash spread. This is not true, however, according to some experts. The reason the rash spreads has nothing to do with the blisters. It has a whole lot to do with coming in contact with anything that the poisonous plant touched, clothing, shoes, backpack, your skin. You sat on your bed to remove the ivy infected jeans. Took a shower. Then sat on your bed to dress in clean clothes. Uh, oh! Several days later you got blisters on your bootie. How did they get there?

Sometimes your body comes under attack by foreign invaders—viruses, bacteria, and fungus. These intruders cause all kinds of dermal problems. Cold sores break out around the mouth, so you can't even hide the hideous, drooling lumps. Thank you, virus. How about scabby, oozing sores on the face called impetigo? Thank you, bacteria. And then we can appreciate a fungus for patchy marks called ringworm of the scalp. Nope, ringworm is not a worm at all. Thank you, fungus.

No matter what the style or type of rash, you would prefer not to have any at all. The bad news about rashes is that you will probably get one. The good news about rashes is that many go away on their own. And if they refuse to leave, doctors can give you medicines to force them to go away. No more rash. Until next time.

TONGUES

Parrot tongues are fat and round.

Cat tongues are scratchy. Long and drippy describe dog tongues. Cow tongues are huge. Frog tongues are fast, very fast. Human tongues are flat and wiggly.

You probably haven't thought much about how disgusting your tongue is. If you were to walk down the street and find a tongue on the side-walk, you would exclaim, "What is that pink, icky lump? Flat and round on one end then it grows into a large blob. Eeuuw, it has little bumps all over one side. I wouldn't want to touch it." Yet, your tongue is constantly a part of your life—touching your lips and mouth; wagging about forming sounds; lifting and flopping to help you to eat. It is almost as though it has a life of its own, like a giant slug living in your mouth.

Basically, a tongue is a large muscle with a layer of mucus over the top. The tongue is the most agile organ in your whole body. Funny, if a person is a gymnast or a dancer, people will say he is agile. But your teacher never comments on how agile your tongue is when you talk during class.

Say "tongue." Say it again and notice your tongue movement. Tongue is a great word for this flexible muscle, since it takes all kinds of maneuvers just to say its own name. Okay, so the tongue is really a large, mucus-layered muscle with a whole bunch of nerves attached. The nerves help you to contort your tongue so that you can talk. They also allow you to notice cold, hot, smooth, rough, wet, dry, and pain.

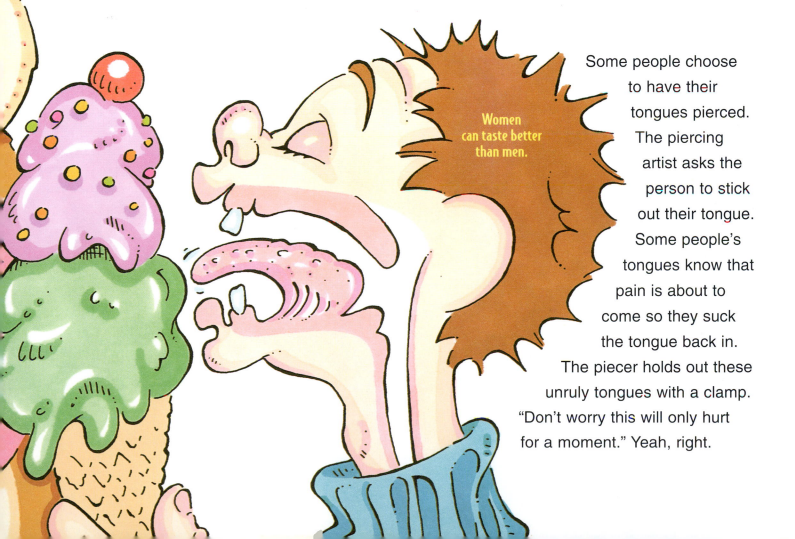

Women can taste better than men.

Some people choose to have their tongues pierced. The piercing artist asks the person to stick out their tongue. Some people's tongues know that pain is about to come so they suck the tongue back in. The piercer holds out these unruly tongues with a clamp. "Don't worry this will only hurt for a moment." Yeah, right.

Fred dreads big bright red bed bugs.

Phil flips for flashy fish fins

Rubber baby buggy bumpers.

Tongue

She sells seashells by the seashore.

Your tongue is attached to the bottom of your mouth by a membrane, called the lingual frenulum, that runs down the center. This membrane is important because it stops you from swallowing your tongue. And swallowing is one of the things that a tongue does best. Without your tongue you couldn't swallow at all. Your tongue rolls your food into a **bolus (bowl-us)**. At swallow time, your tongue lifts up, shoves the bolus into the back of your mouth, and sends food and liquid down your food tube. In some people the lingual frenulum is too short so the tongue movements are limited. It makes it hard for the person to talk and they are said to be tongue-tied. Doctors fix tongue-tied people by cutting the membrane. **Ouch!**

Twisters

Shelly tells Shirley she's silly to sail so slow.

THE SIXTH SICK SHEIK'S SIXTH SHEEP'S SICK.

Bill bets Brad brown bread is better buttered.

The skunk sat on a stump; the skunk thunk the stump stunk, but the stump thunk the skunk stunk.

The only letter sounds that your can say without using your tongue are m, p, f, and v.

Stick out your tongue and check out the surface. Better yet, ask your brother or sister to stick out his or her tongue and study the surface. The top of the tongue is loaded with little bumps. Most people call these lumps your taste buds. **However, they are actually called papillae (puh-PILL-ee).** Papillae comes from the Latin word for pimple. Surrounding each papilla is a moat like those around a castle. Along the edges of each moat are the actual taste buds. Each papilla contains anywhere from one to two hundred taste buds. The food you eat is dissolved in your spit. The spittle dribbles from the papilla into the moat, hits your taste buds and Wha-la! You taste pizza.

Actually, your tongue only recognizes four different tastes: bitter, sour, sweet, and salty. Different parts of your tongue are more sensitive to certain tastes. The tip of your tongue likes sweet and salt. The sides of your tongue like sour. And the very back notices bitter. The center of your tongue doesn't do much tasting. So, to taste something like pizza, your brain and tongue work together to combine the different tastes into flavors.

HOLD THAT TONGUE

What you need:
You and your tongue.

What you do:
Stick out your tongue. Hold onto the tip of your tongue with your fingers.

Say the alphabet. Try to not move your lips. Notice how tongue-tied you've become?

Sing "Mary Had a Little Lamb" or another favorite tune while holding your tongue.

Now, go ask your grandmother to sing "Twinkle, Twinkle Little Star" while holding her tongue.

Ever notice that food just doesn't taste the same when your nose is stuffed up? Your nose and mouth together help you to taste. Inside your head, nose, mouth, and throat are interconnected by a bunch of passages. The tiny molecules from baking peanut butter cookies float through the air. You breathe them in. The cookie molecules pass over the taste buds on the back of your tongue. The food molecules dissolve in the saliva and you actually taste the cookies without putting them into your mouth. Yummy! Air cookies! So, you can actually taste smells.

That's good for nice smells. But what about yucky smells? Yes, well, it means that you have actually tasted those icky smells. To be honest, you have at least had a little taste as the doggie dookie smell passed your taste buds. How lovely. Maybe you have eaten something nasty and exclaimed, **"This tastes like poop!"** Then your cousin responds, "How do you know? Have you eaten poop?" You could just explain the whole smell and taste thing. Then say, "You have eaten poop, too." That may keep your bratty cousin quiet . . . for a little while anyway.

THE SMELL CONNECTION

What you need:
A stick of mint gum, and yourself.

What you do:
Wash your hands, then unwrap the stick of gum. With one hand, pinch your nose tightly so that all smells are blocked.

With your other hand, place the stick of gum in your mouth.

While still holding your nose, chew the gum eight times. What do you taste?

Release your nose hold. Whoa! A tasteful.

If your heard someone say that your Aunt Jackie had an itchy tongue, it doesn't mean she should go to the doctor. An "itching tongue" is an old saying for someone anxious to repeat gossip.

72

VARICOSE VEINS

Very close veins mostly appear in older people.

Isn't it varicose veins? Yes, but "very close veins" is an accurate description. Okay, think very close but say varicose. Varicose comes from the Latin word *varix*, which means a dilated vein. Funny, how so many "v" words are used for blood stuff like vein, vessel, vascular, valve, and varicose. Varicose veins form from weak vascular vessel valves. Quickly say that three times. How very vexing!

You may nicely ask your Great-Aunt Sally or your Great-Uncle George if they have varicose veins. Should they show you, in your mind silently say, *Geez, that is so disgusting. I hope I don't ever get those.* But aloud say, "Thank you, that's very interesting." Most of the time, people don't like to show off their varicose veins, so you might have to settle with sneaking a peek when you encounter an elder on the beach.

Veins are a very important part of your circulatory system. Basically, this system is a pump and a bunch of tubes. The pump is your heart. The tubes are your arteries, capillaries, and veins.

The arteries deliver enriched blood out of the heart to the body. The heart shoves the blood to help it on its way. You can feel the push in the arteries when you take your pulse. The arteries get smaller and smaller until only one blood cell can pass through at a time. The artery is now a capillary. Once the blood has passed around all of its oxygen and nutrients, it must go back to the lungs for refueling. The veins are the route back to the heart. By now, all of the pressure from the pump is gone. The blood moves slower. For the veins above your heart, gravity helps pull the blood down. For veins below your heart, little one-way valves keep the blood from running back down to collect in your ankles.

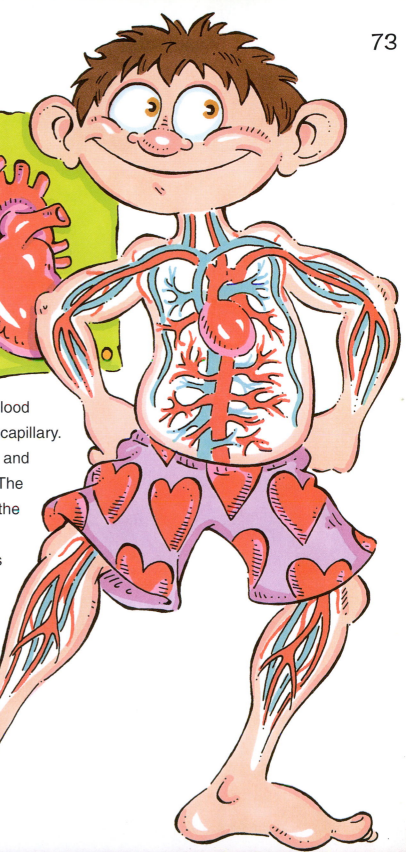

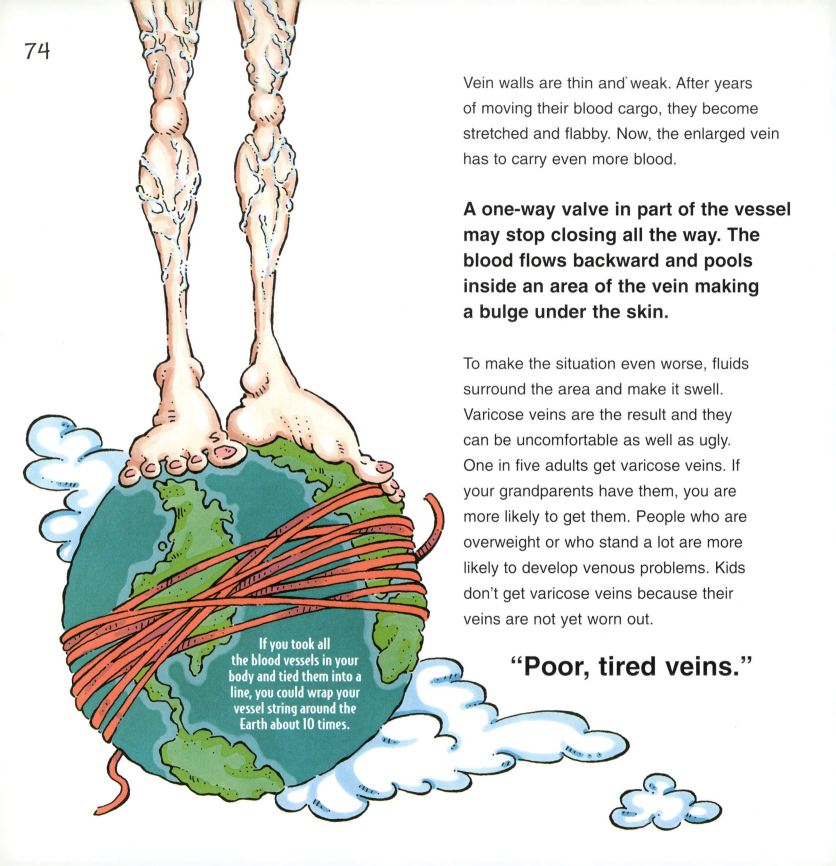

If you took all the blood vessels in your body and tied them into a line, you could wrap your vessel string around the Earth about 10 times.

Vein walls are thin and weak. After years of moving their blood cargo, they become stretched and flabby. Now, the enlarged vein has to carry even more blood.

A one-way valve in part of the vessel may stop closing all the way. The blood flows backward and pools inside an area of the vein making a bulge under the skin.

To make the situation even worse, fluids surround the area and make it swell. Varicose veins are the result and they can be uncomfortable as well as ugly. One in five adults get varicose veins. If your grandparents have them, you are more likely to get them. People who are overweight or who stand a lot are more likely to develop venous problems. Kids don't get varicose veins because their veins are not yet worn out.

"Poor, tired veins."

VEIN COVERUP!

GET THOSE UNSIGHTLY VESSELS!

VASCULAR SUPPLEMENTS!

VARICOSE CREAMS

ON A VEINY DAY

What you need: Your tongue, a mirror

What you do: Make sure the mirror is in a well-lit room. Touch your tongue to the top of your mouth and thrust it out. Check it out in the mirror. Yes, you look rather silly, but notice the vessels under your tongue. The tiny lines are capillaries. The pink tubes are arteries. The big blue lines are veins. How many veins do you see? Now go check out the underside of your little sister's tongue. Does it look similar? How about your babysitter's tongue or mail carrier's tongue?

VITAVEINS VITAMINS

VANISH THOSE VEINS!

AMAZINGLY SEE VEINS DISAPPEAR!

Some people swear by Horse Chestnut pills. Miracle cures for varicose veins may abound because the actual treatments for getting rid of them are pretty gruesome. In one type of surgery, cuts are made along the vein and surgical hooks snag and fish out the vein. **Vein stripping** is as creepy as it sounds. Incisions are made at the groin and the lower leg. The long leg vein is then tied off and pulled out of the leg. "Euwwww!" **Sclerotherapy** injects medications into the veins to seal them shut and stop the blood flow. Over time the vein shrinks and breaks down. Many folks just choose to use support stockings that bind up the legs. Support stockings are not a cure but take away vein pain.

WARTS

Okay, admit it.

You have one—

a **W A R T**.

Even the word, "wart," sounds disgusting. Warts are ugly, little, cauliflowerlike growths that sprout on the surface of skin. Ugly, of course, unless you are a male wart hog. Male wart hogs are tusked hogs native to parts of Africa. The male wart hog is endowed with warts on the cheeks and between the eyes and tusks. Who knows? Maybe the female wart hog is attracted to the male with the largest and the most warts.

Although facial warts are common on male wart hogs, in humans warts usually take root on the hands, fingers, elbows, and feet. But they can show up almost anywhere. Storybook witches and goblins have nose warts. This is not a common place for warts to grow.

The scientific name for a wart is verruca (va-ROO-ka) vulgaris. Very fitting, as the word vulgar can actually mean gross.

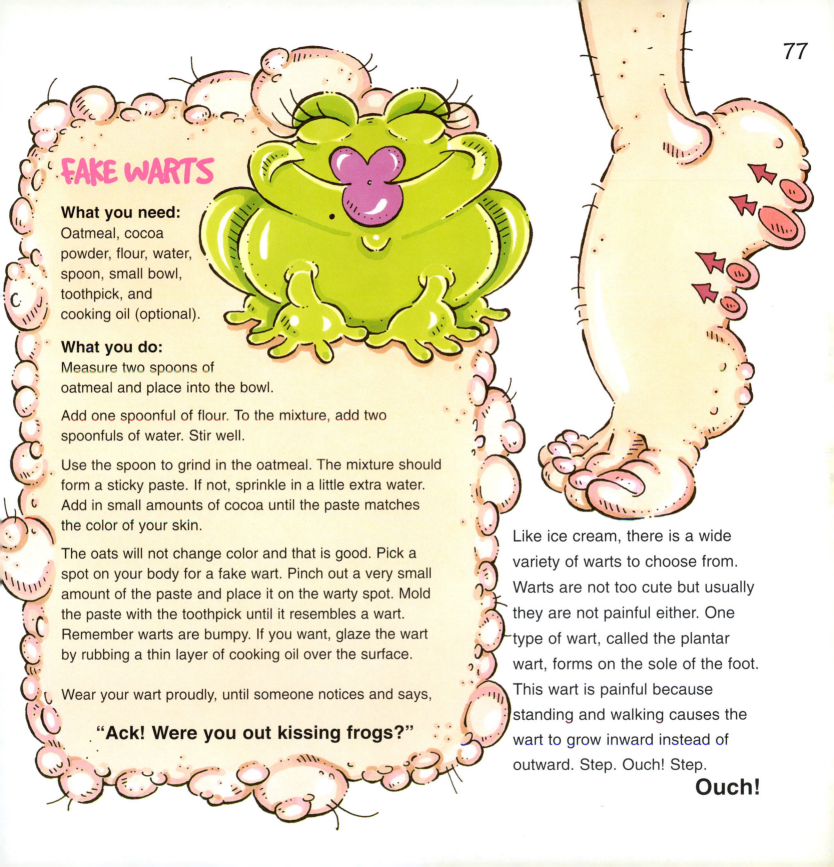

FAKE WARTS

What you need:
Oatmeal, cocoa powder, flour, water, spoon, small bowl, toothpick, and cooking oil (optional).

What you do:
Measure two spoons of oatmeal and place into the bowl.

Add one spoonful of flour. To the mixture, add two spoonfuls of water. Stir well.

Use the spoon to grind in the oatmeal. The mixture should form a sticky paste. If not, sprinkle in a little extra water. Add in small amounts of cocoa until the paste matches the color of your skin.

The oats will not change color and that is good. Pick a spot on your body for a fake wart. Pinch out a very small amount of the paste and place it on the warty spot. Mold the paste with the toothpick until it resembles a wart. Remember warts are bumpy. If you want, glaze the wart by rubbing a thin layer of cooking oil over the surface.

Wear your wart proudly, until someone notices and says,

"Ack! Were you out kissing frogs?"

Like ice cream, there is a wide variety of warts to choose from. Warts are not too cute but usually they are not painful either. One type of wart, called the plantar wart, forms on the sole of the foot. This wart is painful because standing and walking causes the wart to grow inward instead of outward. Step. Ouch! Step.

Ouch!

Innocent toads have taken the blame for causing warts. "Hey, if you pick up that toad, you will get warts." Maybe toads started this rumor so that people would leave them alone. Warts are actually caused by a virus. A virus is a little germ that gets on your skin if you touch somewhere that it hangs out. The wart viruses climb onto your skin, get comfortable, multiply, and form the little bumpy growths. Unlike toads, you can't see viruses, so it is hard to look out for them. But you can encounter wart viruses by touching warty areas and by walking barefoot on warty floors, such as in locker rooms or shower stalls. So, don't go stroking your friends warts and wear foot coverings in high wart areas.

Silly Wart Cures Through the Ages

1. Rub warts with pebbles. Throw the pebbles into a grave.

2. Rub warts with the blood from a black-feathered chicken.

3. Rub warts with the hand of a dead person.

4. Take a nail from out of a coffin. Scratch the wart with the coffin nail until the wart bleeds.

5. Rub the wart with a bone. Set the bone down where you picked it up. Walk away from the bone without looking back.

Given enough time, most warts go away all by themselves. Sometimes the wart hangs out for several weeks but there are a few stubborn ones that may stay for several years. You could try purchasing wart cream from the drugstore, but most of them have limited results in getting rid of warts. (Or you could try covering the wart for a week with several layers of adhesive tape; remove the tape on the seventh day for twelve hours; cover again for a week).

If this doesn't work, doctors can remove swollen, painful warts. Foot doctors, or **podiatrists (poh-DIE-a-trists)** have the great honor of removing many plantar warts.

Warts are most often removed by freezing them with liquid nitrogen, electrocuting them with low voltage, or burning them with acid.

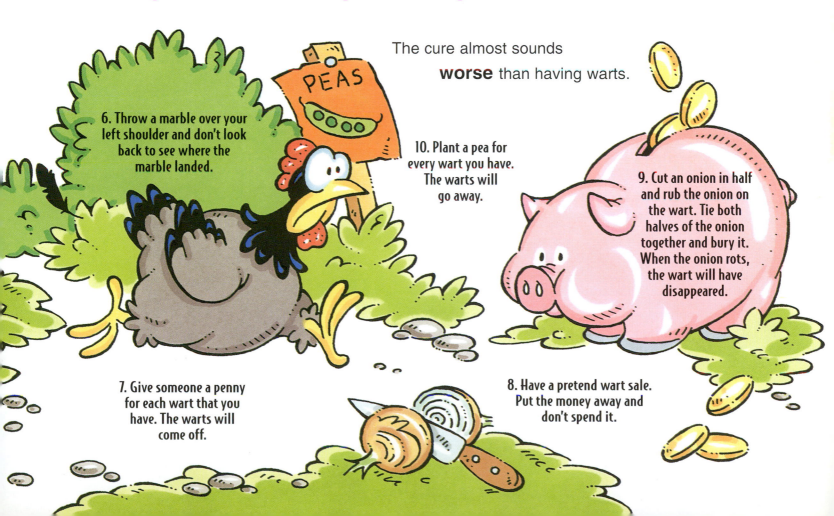

The cure almost sounds **worse** than having warts.

PEAS

6. Throw a marble over your left shoulder and don't look back to see where the marble landed.

10. Plant a pea for every wart you have. The warts will go away.

9. Cut an onion in half and rub the onion on the wart. Tie both halves of the onion together and bury it. When the onion rots, the wart will have disappeared.

7. Give someone a penny for each wart that you have. The warts will come off.

8. Have a pretend wart sale. Put the money away and don't spend it.

Hey, Good News! More GROSSOLOGY® Books!

THE END

WoW! Don't miss these other incredibly disgusting Grossology titles! (They should be available at whatever bookstore you like to visit. If not, the bookstore can always order them for you. Enjoy!)

GROSSOLOGY

The original gross classic! Sometimes it's crusty. Sometimes it's stinky. And sometimes it's slimy. Not the book—your body! And here's all the icky, oozing information about it, presented in the scientifically correct manner that has already grossed out millions.

ANIMAL GROSSOLOGY

Just when you thought it was safe, Grossology is back with a look at the most repulsive habbits of our animal friends. You'll learn about slimy creatures, vomit munchers, blood suckers, and unforgettable animal poops.

GROSSOLOGY BEGINS AT HOME

Yup, there's a whole world of grossness right under your nose. Or behind your bed. Or between your toes. Or . . . you get the idea. Your home is the perfect laboratory for the science of really putrid things. So take a tour of your very own little house of yuckiness with Grossology as your guide.